Date Due

THE OLD GLORY

Books by Robert Lowell

THE OLD GLORY
IMITATIONS
PHAEDRA *(translation)*
LIFE STUDIES
THE MILLS OF THE KAVANAUGHS
LORD WEARY'S CASTLE
LAND OF UNLIKENESS

Robert Lowell
The Old Glory

FARRAR, STRAUS & GIROUX   *New York*

The *Introduction* by Robert Brustein is used by permission of the author and Columbia Records. Copyright © 1965 by Columbia Records. All rights reserved. From the Columbia Records original cast recording of *Benito Cereno*.

The *Director's Note* by Jonathan Miller is used by permission of the author and The New York Times. Copyright © 1964 by The New York Times Company.

My Kinsman, Major Molineux was published originally in *Partisan Review; Benito Cereno* appeared originally in *Show* Magazine.

To Jonathan Miller
and Randall Jarrell

My sources have been Nathaniel Hawthorne's stories and sketches, *Endecott and the Red Cross, The Maypole at Merry Mount* and *My Kinsman, Major Molineux;* Thomas Morton's *New Canaan;* and Herman Melville's *Benito Cereno.*

R.L.

Contents

Introduction

Benito Cereno is the third play in the extraordinary theater trilogy by Robert Lowell called *The Old Glory,* a work in which the renowned poet has fashioned a dramatic history of the American character. Held together by the unifying symbol of the flag, *The Old Glory* is based on stories by Hawthorne and a novella by Melville, but while Mr. Lowell has managed to adapt these tales with relative fidelity to the original texts, he has made them wholly and uniquely his own work. Invested with the author's keen historical sense and marvelous gift for language, the source materials assume the thickness and authority of myth; ritual and metaphors abound; traditional literature and historical events begin to function like Greek mythology, as the source and reflection of contemporary behavior. Mr. Lowell feels the past working in his very bones. And it is his subtle achievement not only to have evoked this past, but also to have superimposed the present upon it, so that the plays manage to look forward and backward at the same time. Adopting a style which is purposely chilling, measured and remote, he has endowed his plays with flinty intelligence and tautened passion, making them work on the spectator with all the suggestive power of non-discursive poems.

The three plays examine the American character at three different points in its historical development. This character the author finds to be permeated with violence from its beginnings—a violence which invariably erupts out in moments of panic. In *Endecott and the Red Cross,* a mild-mannered Puritan military man, faced with high-living Anglican-Royalists in colonial America, is forced into shedding blood by political-religious expediency; and in *My Kinsman, Major Molineux,* the American Revolution unfolds as a violent nightmare experienced by two Deerfield youths seeking out their British cousin in Boston, "the city of the dead."

In *Benito Cereno,* the third and finest play, Mr. Lowell brings us to the beginning of the 19th century and proceeds to unearth the seeds of our current discords. Based on Herman Melville's novella of the same name, *Benito Cereno* has all the theatrical power of the first two plays, as well as a heavily charged prose style and a strong suspenseful narrative. Melville's story is largely concerned with the shadow cast over a civilized mind by the primitive darkness. Mr. Lowell heightens this theme, examining along the way the ambiguous American attitude towards slavery and servitude.

In the American Place Theatre production, Jonathan Miller, the director, paced this play with an eye to its half-languorous, half-ominous atmosphere, giving it the rhythm of "an ocean undulating in long scoops of swells," but finally letting it explode into a shocking climax, to the accompaniment of discharging muskets. The visual effects of the original production, with its simple set and illustrative costuming, were excellent (the crisp uniforms of the American officers in black cutaway coats and white tights juxtaposed against the shabby-sumptuous attire of Cereno and the rags of the slaves). But it is the acting that was really unusual. In an age of flaccid, self-indulgent histrionics, Mr. Miller evoked performances of extraordinary depth, control and energy. Three actors in particular were superb: Roscoe Lee Browne, alternating between Calypso sunniness and sinister threat as Babu; Lester Rawlins, suave, smug and self-satisfied as Delano; and Frank Langella as Cereno, his eyes continually lowered with shame, his voice morose and rich, a trembling wreck of stateliness and nobility. But it is a violation to single out individuals for praise when the entire cast was functioning with that precision and power that we have come to expect only from long-established repertory companies.

The Old Glory, certainly, is the first American play to utilize historical materials in a compelling theatrical manner (just compare it with those lifeless high-school pageants that Maxwell Anderson used to grind out), perhaps because it is the first such play to assume a mature intellect on the part of its audience. After years of prosaic language, mundane forms and retarded themes—obstacles which only O'Neill was able to transcend successfully in his last plays, and then only through sheer doggedness and will—the American drama has finally developed an important subject and an eloquent voice. *The Old Glory* may well mark the beginning of a dramatic renaissance in America, during which our theater—like our fiction and poetry—will be able to tap the sources of our inmost being, and not just sink us deeper into narcosis and complacency. *Benito Cereno* is a cultural-poetic masterpiece, but the entire trilogy is an event of great moment. For it heralds the arrival not just of a brilliant new dramatist but of one who may very well come to revolutionize the American theater.

ROBERT BRUSTEIN

Director's note

I think it was John Locke, the English philosopher, who defined property as that with which a man hath mixed his labor. By that token, in directing Robert Lowell's *The Old Glory*, I feel that I have a small stake in the United States of America.

When I last came to America, I came with an English show, *Beyond the Fringe*, grafted a piece of my own country onto the fat carcass of Broadway and did very nicely thank you. But there was no mixture with America in it at all, and while I enjoyed the experience I always felt that I was on the outside looking in. *The Old Glory* changed all that, however. For the first time I was able to work with a great American writer and also had the chance of mixing my labor with nearly one hundred American theatrical workmen.

The play was mounted in an unusual way. It was a great poet's first entry into the theater and at the same time we were in on the start of a new dramatic experiment, which actually involved building the premises while we were rehearsing. It was the most extraordinary example of mass cooperation that I have ever known. During the nine weeks of casting and rehearsals I kept searching for a satisfactory metaphor to describe all this and I finally saw it in terms of *Treasure Island*.

Lowell was like Jim Hawkins, who had inherited a strange treasure map. His text was full of exotic instructions and rich proposals, all pointing the way to some unprecedented reward of new drama. With this chart in my hands I signed on the crew of actors, musicians and designers while the keel of our *Hispaniola* was being laid in the nave of St. Clement's Church. The whole adventure came as a delicious shock which unfolded more and more unexpected pleasures as the weeks went by. For I had been warned before coming back to the States that American actors were incapable of playing with the necessary formal high style which Lowell's text demanded, and that no American cast could subordinate its egotism to the stringent requirements of meticulous ensemble playing.

I had been told also that Americans were incapable of beautiful diction. This was especially alarming in *Benito Cereno,* since Lowell had written long swells of superb verse which called for an almost operatic vocal mastery. Once again, my fears proved groundless. Lester Rawlins, Frank Langella, and Roscoe Lee Browne rose magnificently to the occasion and startled even the author with the rich, complex possibilities of his own writing. Along with Jack Ryland the four worked together like a string quartet that had rehearsed in collaboration for years. There was also the cast of Negro extras who worked together with a fierce conscientiousness which I had never seen before on the American stage.

Looking back in pleasure over all this, I can only repeat what I must have said over and over again to the cast of these two plays. That is was an honor and a privilege to work with such noble and talented people.

xvi

Director's Note

These are difficult plays to mount and I only arrived at what seemed to me to be an entirely satisfactory solution with the last two pieces in the trilogy. The first play presents the most awkward puzzles for a director who has to marry scenes of ritual festivity with long passages of contemplative recitative. The essence of "Endecott and the Red Cross" seems to me to be its complex spiritual irony, and this can be easily swamped by the spectacle of the mid-summer fête. In the first production we never entirely got over this problem and after a lot of rehearsal, cutting and re-writing, we had to drop the play before the first night which seriously damaged the grand design. But it is possible that this play needs to be expanded anyway and presented as a full length piece on its own.

My Kinsman, Major Molineux is the most stylized of the three plays and it needs to be put across with scintillating artificiality. The costume designer, Willa Kim, and I worked on the basic idea of the 18th century political cartoon which dramatized the violent fervour of the times and gave it an almost surrealist nightmare sting. We painted the actors chalk grey and dressed them in costumes made of stiff unbleached cotton. The pockets and embroidery were drawn on in black ink so that the cast looked like pieces of paper cut out of a coffee-house broadsheet. Everyone except Robin and his brother was then very strictly choreographed so that they came and went like crude putty coloured marionettes. The controlling image for all this was Alice-in-Wonderland—as if the flesh and blood Deerfield boys had wandered into a dream world of sloganeering playing cards. When Molineux is struck down at the end his crude features should suddenly and shockingly leak scarlet

xvii

blood. Somewhere in the revolutionary crowd I put a corpse in a winding sheet as if the hot wind of revolution had wakened the dead. Gilray and Lewis Carroll are the figures to keep in mind here.

I was driven by two ideas for *Benito Cereno*, the last play. First, as regards staging and diction, it seemed to me that Lowell had written an opera without music and the four principal actors were directed to move and speak as if they were soloists in an oratorio and they should be placed on the stage as if they were delivering Mozartian quartets and duets—very formal with no restless modern naturalism. This play seemed to me to be like a new *Tempest* with the Spanish captain playing a sort of drugged Prospero held captive by his Negro Babu. This idea turns the Spanish boat into a black magic island where all the normal laws of nature and society are relaxed and paralysed. The vision of the American captain is blurred by the heat, the lethargy and the exotic languor of the Negro slaves. Everything in this production must be bent towards creating this sense of lethargy. The Negroes need only to be seen on stage in ones and twos, mending nets and so on, unless otherwise indicated. Then from time to time they should all hum on one note in unison so as to create a vague off stage murmur like hives on a summer day. The entertainment should be baroque and courtly with no concession made to modern nightclub negritude. By the end of it, Delano should be sent off into a trance of drowsy reminiscence, as if Odysseus had succumbed after all in the palace of Circe. When final violence comes it should puncture the poisoned atmosphere which ought to have been slowly and lingeringly inflated throughout the evening. Finally, when everything

is still on the deck, Babu dead, and Delano upright amongst
the bloody debris, a Negro girl should come on stage slowly,
pause and give a long, awkward ghastly scream—like a
wounded albatross.

JONATHAN MILLER

The Old Glory, as produced at The American Place Theatre, was the winner of five Obie Awards for the 1964-65 season, including Best Play.

ENDECOTT &
THE RED CROSS

Endecott and the Red Cross

In order of appearance

Mr. Blackstone

Thomas Morton

Edward

Edith

Sergeant

Soldier

Governor Endecott

Elder Palfrey

Soldiers

Indians

Revellers: Maskers, dancers, people of Merry Mount

The scene

In the 1630's, Merry Mount, the settlement of Thomas Morton near Wollaston, Massachusetts.

To one side, a Maypole covered with fresh birch branches and tied with ribbons of twenty different colors. In the background, a little to one side, the front of a brown 17th Century house with diamond windows. A small group of REVELLERS is trying on animal heads: wolves, stags, etc. In the middle ground, a fine young man with a rainbow scarf; with him, a beautiful woman in a rainbow-colored dress. They are EDWARD and EDITH, just married and chosen King and Queen of the May, for it is the First of May. A MAN comes out and sloppily attaches a flag, the Red Cross of England, above the doorway. In the foreground, two men are talking. They are THOMAS MORTON, the head of the settlement, and MR. BLACKSTONE, an Episcopal minister, just arrived from England. MORTON wears a shabby coffee-colored suit, part cloth and part deerskin. He is overweight and his manner with the minister is complacent, oily and conciliatory. MR. BLACKSTONE is dressed in a finely fitting black minister's habit. He has long set cavalier hair and talks with the crisp briskness of a high official addressing an inferior.

MR. BLACKSTONE

I don't know why I am here at Merry Mount.

These hills don't look like hills; they are too blue;
the ocean is even bluer,
there are three thousand miles of it between me and home,
between here and Oxford and my King.
I wonder why he picked me for this mission.

MORTON

We are strange co-conspirators, your Reverence.

MR. BLACKSTONE

I don't understand you, Mr. Morton.

MORTON

We've got to see that God and King
get their money's worth out of this colony—
God and King and Mr. Morton.

MR. BLACKSTONE

I suppose we'll have to work together.
I wonder why Archbishop Laud chose me.
I am a specialist in Church of England ritual.
This is my first taste of authority.

MORTON

Authority! Bite on it! You'll love it!
Authority is the only appetite that grows younger with age.

MR. BLACKSTONE

I certainly don't love America.
I'm used to prepared ground.
I put the final polish on a parish that is already polished.

MORTON

Oh, America is God's land. Even the blue-assed Puritans
can't change that!

6

If you stay here and open your eyes, you'll love it.
Look at me, I know its animals, its birds,
and every inch and inlet of this coast,
as far south as Plymouth and as far north as Salem.

MR. BLACKSTONE

I'm not a bird-watcher or an Indian, Mr. Morton.
I don't see the point of this outpost of England.

MORTON

There's money in it, your Reverence.
Furs and adventure and God knows what!
Come down to earth with us, Sir!
I felt as you do when I first came here:
no plays, cathedrals, or learning.
But you'll get used to us. I need you officially.
I want you to crown Edward and Edith King and Queen
  of the May.

MR. BLACKSTONE

I have just married them,
that's as far as my office goes.
I have serious work to do, Mr. Morton!

MAN WITH A STAG'S HEAD

[*In a high comical voice*]

We need a real Church of England man to give us a true
  King and Queen.

REVELLERS

Give us our King and Queen!

MORTON

You see how much we want you.

EDWARD

Make me a king, your Reverence.

MR. BLACKSTONE

A true king rules by divine right,
he is born king, not made one by clergy.

[*Wearily*]

Come, Edward, I crown you May-King.
Edith, I crown you May-Queen.

REVELLERS

Hurrah for King Edward and Queen Edith!
Hurrah for the King and Queen of England!

MR. BLACKSTONE

Now that the coronation is over,
I hope you'll excuse me. I have letters to write to England.

MORTON

Why, Mr. Blackstone,
you are neglecting your parish!
My children are breaking in the wilderness for you.

[*In a loud voice*]

Put on your heads, my children,
and be the animals you are.
Dance round and round the Maypole,
and show our pastor what life is made for.
I'll read you my new verses.

[*Reads in a buffoonish sing-song while the* REVELLERS *put on their animal heads and dance an antic and somewhat obscene dance around the Maypole*]

8

I've whiskey and gin
to make your heads spin,
like a drumming drum
or a barrel of rum,
when the King and Queen come.
I've wolves and stags,
and men in rags
to kiss the long throat
and beaver coat
of any free maid,
be she white or red—
in the forest, or in her bed . . .

[*A few* WHITE *and* INDIAN GIRLS *dance onto the stage*]

MR. BLACKSTONE

Enough, Mr. Morton!
This sort of thing won't do!

MORTON

You're right, your Reverence.
You're an Oxford man, you'll smooth up my verses.

MR. BLACKSTONE

You misunderstand me, Mr. Morton!
I wasn't sent here by his Lordship of Canterbury
to smooth up your horrible doggerel.
There must be some decency,
there must be some boundary between the Indian and
    English subjects.
Our bishops are busy working out a suitable formula
to express the King's wishes on the matter.

9

Unless this clowning and disorder stop, Sir,
your royal patronage will be withdrawn.

MORTON

Right you are, your Reverence. This is easily fixed.

[*In a loud voice*]

Children, I want you to dance like ladies and gentlemen.
Dismiss your Indian companions,
remember you represent the Crown on this frontier.
Dance for England!
I will sing you a song.

[*As* MORTON *sings, the* INDIAN GIRLS *steal away, the* OTHER
REVELLERS *take off their animal heads and dance a very sedate
and stately dance*]

Fair and fair, and twice so fair,
As fair as any may be,
The fairest shepherd on our green,
A love for any lady.

[EDWARD *leads the dance*]

Fair and fair, and twice so fair,
Listen to cupid's curse:
All they who change old love for new,
Pray God they change for worse.

[EDITH *leads the dance*]

England's our old love, your Reverence.
We know we'll never change, don't we?

MR. BLACKSTONE

A very pretty dance, Mr. Morton!
I don't like your ribaldry,
You are very changeable and double-faced here.

MORTON

The world's like a playing card now,
black and white checkered squares on the back,
a king in all his theatrical pomp in front.

MR. BLACKSTONE

Black and white checkers?
You are quite wrong;
the world is now a pyramid. Our King stands at the top,
below him his subjects descend uniformly
down to the lowest farmer.
If you don't understand the principles of our pyramid,
you'll only be an obstruction to us.

MORTON

Authority is already growing on you—
you speak to me like a school teacher.
This hurts me. I am running a plantation,
not preaching a Latin oration before the King at Oxford.
The King has very few friends here.
I don't see your Oxford graduates volunteering by
        the hundreds
to support King Charles here in the wilderness!

MR. BLACKSTONE

Their talents are needed in England.
I told you we are building a pyramid
that will descend from the King down to the lowest farmer.

MORTON

That is your theory. I have mine for this country.
Lords and college men are needed in England, I'm
        needed here.

I have to walk on a razor's edge between the Indians
and Governor Endecott's Puritan settlement in Salem.
I have a plantation, I have to make it pay.

MR. BLACKSTONE

Our King understands your talents, Mr. Morton,
he is preparing a position of great honor for you.
When I read the royal proclamation to the Puritans,
your troubles will be over.

MORTON

Ho! a limb of Satan! That's what the Puritans
will call your useful Royal Governor.

MR. BLACKSTONE

Poor things, the Royal Governor will indeed fall on them
    like a thunderbolt!

MORTON

I'm sure he will. I suppose there'll be a very useful Bishop.

MR. BLACKSTONE

Of course, there'll be a Bishop.
I see what you are hinting at—
God preserve me from the office!

MORTON

Oh, no, we need you. You have the right presence.
You will fall on the Puritans like a thunderbolt.
I have one more question:
I suppose the King will be sending a standing army over,
a regiment or so to keep the Puritans in a good humor?
That might be the most useful export of all.

MR. BLACKSTONE

Oh, the King has soldiers,
if the church should need them.

MORTON

None to spare on America, I guess;
he needs that sort of talent in England.
I hear there's been church trouble in Scotland.

MR. BLACKSTONE

Just talk!

MORTON

I never knew a man so short of cash as King Charles!

MR. BLACKSTONE

That will be over in a year or two,
When the Archbishop has thoroughly installed our Church,
no one will lift a finger against the King.
The kingdom will pay, as you say of your plantation.

MORTON

That'll be a new world! Quite a change!
Right now you have all the machinery set up:
The King, Archbishops, Bishops, governor-generals,
governors, clerks, offices, titles, etc.:
but there's no money.
England's like a full-rigged ship in a dead calm.
But I'm sure your religion will settle all that.
I like religion,
we need all the right religion we can get at Merry Mount.
God knows, I've sweated to uphold the Church of England
in this dominion, but the Puritans,

13

excuse me, Sir, have made a hog-sty of my plantation.
They hate me and keep manhandling me,
because I love the Book of Common Prayer.
The Book of Common Prayer is a great book,
I read it night and day to my family—
I call these people my family,
I am their father.

MR. BLACKSTONE

The Puritans must have something else on you
besides your love for the Book of Common Prayer.

MORTON

Well, they don't care for our May Day.
There's no harm in our traditional May Day,
it comes down to us, I guess, from King Arthur.
It's one of those things that makes England England
and survives a hundred civil wars and rulers.
You can't expect my fellows to change all that—
your Reverence, they want you to marry them,
they have been standing on tiptoe up here
for months waiting for your ship and May Day.
We only need good wives to keep the Ten Commandments.

MR. BLACKSTONE

Your May Day and a few other things
will have to be toned down a bit.
You're not suggesting that the Puritans will defy the King?
The King is beyond criticism.

MORTON

I see. You're saying that I am the only fly in the
    King's butter.

Well, I probably am. Still, these kings,
they come and go with us.
They come and go, but England remains.

MR. BLACKSTONE

Would anything remain of England
if a Puritan were King?
A man like your Governor Endecott?
I am talking nonsense,
but such horrors have happened on the Continent.

MORTON

Oh, England would survive that little diversion
We'd have men singing psalms through their noses
and marching and counter-marching across the realm
    in iron.
Then their dust would blow off,
and we'd again have our May Days and bishops.

MR. BLACKSTONE

Well, that won't happen:
our Church and our King are in the saddle.
At last there's no contradiction
between loyalty, truth and power.
Do you think your Governor Endecott will defy
    the Crown?

MORTON

I don't know. I know this, though:
Endecott is an Englishman, he carried our flag, the Red
    Cross of
England, against the Spaniard. He'll never defy England,
he's as loyal there as I am.

MR. BLACKSTONE

Yes, you are both double-faced,
though of course I know you've only been playing
with trivial things such as loose morals,
while Endecott is mixed up with blasphemy and treason.
I hear he was a courtier and lettered man in England,
but that here he is the Puritan of the Puritans.

MORTON

Yes, he's their brass bull snorting fire.
We talk a lot about Endecott, but can't figure him out.
He's not one of those bone-headed, ignorant preachers
who thinks creation began in his pulpit;
but he talks worse than any of them,
or rather, he doesn't talk, he acts,
and all he does goes against our plans for America.
Still you have to allow a man of principle
a little hypocrisy when he plays with power.
No, your Reverence, Endecott and the Puritans
will never revolt from England.
That would be walking blindfold off a plank into
    the Atlantic.
They're nothing without England.

> [*A* REVELLER *puts a toy hawk on* MORTON's *wrist. It is meant to
> be a real hawk*]

MR. BLACKSTONE

We'll grind their necks down.
That's a fine bird you have on your wrist, Mr. Morton.

MORTON

A bit of England!

I was brought up with gentlemen, men who knew
    their hawks!
I caught this one a fortnight after I landed,
and had him eating out of my hand by Christmas.
Anything worth doing takes taming and planning
and sleight of hand, but these Puritans
run right at anything they want like animals.
They'd die out here in a day without their heavy guns
    and sermons.
I know all about hawks and graceful
roundabout ways of killing.

    [*A gunshot is heard off-stage*]

MR. BLACKSTONE

What's that?—I don't like the sound of guns!

MORTON

Just an Indian. They're rather a head-ache.
When an Indian gets something to drink
he blasts away at anything in sight.
We have to give them liquor and guns
to get their furs;
they're sick of beads and shells.

MR. BLACKSTONE

They ought to keep their shooting out of earshot!
Why don't you set up targets for them
on some deserted beach? I don't like explosions.

MORTON

Right again, your Reverence!
You're the man we want. I've always prayed

for a good Church of England man to come to
    Merry Mount.
You're really saving my life. Imagine thinking
of giving the Indians targets in this game-overrun country!

MR. BLACKSTONE

[*Crisply*]

Our theology teaches us to deal with what's at hand,
    Mr. Morton.
Our administration regards you as at hand,
so henceforth you can spare me your irony,
and also excuse me. I have important letters to write.

[*He goes stiffly into the house*]

MORTON

A queer bird.
He's unimaginably useful to me at this point.

[MORTON *sits stroking his hawk. Two* PURITAN SOLDIERS, *a* SER-
GEANT *and a* PRIVATE, *enter. They are tremendously armed:
matchlocks, gray uniforms, polished iron helmets and breast-
plates*]

MORTON

Who are you standing out there,
gaping at me in iron?
You look like Spaniards from the Low Countries.
You'd better move on. I'm not keeping open-house!

SERGEANT

We come from Governor Endecott. We're his vanguard.
Who are you, Sir?

18

MORTON

I am Thomas Morton, the host of Merry Mount.
I am the big sachem. As a matter of fact,
the Narragansetts have just made me a sachem.

SERGEANT

I knew you were Morton. I just wanted your
    own confession.
We know why you are a sachem, too: you've been selling
guns to the Indians.

SOLDIER

We're here to burn your settlement down.

MORTON

Oh, that old racket! Miles Standish tried it.
It won't work now! I've cleared things in England.
You are conspirators against the King!

SERGEANT

His Excellency, John Endecott, Governor of Salem,
is on the march here. He has more soldiers than you
    can count.
You won't be able to find your settlement when he
    leaves you.

MORTON

You talk like full grown bears now.
I remember when our strength was equal;
you whined like bears' whelps then.
I know you Puritans. You only care for profit;
your holy thirst for mink and beaverskins drives you mad.

SERGEANT

You've been trading the Indians guns and liquor for furs.
They've been killing our women and children.

MORTON

They were probably using your own guns.
Your hands aren't clean! Don't tell me
you give the Indians glass beads and clam shells for
    their furs!

SERGEANT

We are waiting for Governor Endecott.
He has more soldiers than you can count.
We are going to burn your settlement to the ground.

MORTON

Come off it, Sergeant!
We are all Englishmen. There are few enough of us in
    the world.
There's no need for us to run berserk and kill each other.

SERGEANT

What's so English about you?

MORTON

My flag. I must go. Enjoy the air here.
I'm sorry I can't ask you into my house.
If you wait here, you'll get some new ideas.
You may want to count up your soldiers and go back
    to Salem.

[*Goes into the house*]

SERGEANT

He must think he's a preacher,
he can't stop talking!

SOLDIER

Yes, Sir, but may I say something?
I think we are talking too much about the numbers of
    our soldiers.
God is a host.
Here in America, we are in Israel.

SERGEANT

Stop preaching!
Endecott knows the fear of God,
he holds a Bible in his left hand
and a loaded pistol in his right. He needs
a man with my war-experience and black tongue
to beat some shape into you meeting-house
orators and Hebrew psalmists.

SOLDIER

The battlefield is the great meeting-house.
Have you noticed the Governor lately?

SERGEANT

Of course.

SOLDIER

I am his orderly.
Have you noticed how he keeps boasting and complaining
about his armor?
First it's too light and then it's too heavy.
Then he keeps jumping from one subject to another.
I can't follow a man unless he stays on one subject.

SERGEANT

Your subject is religion.

SOLDIER

The Governor has been doing too much thinking.
Do you think he'll burn this settlement down?

SERGEANT

No.

SOLDIER

The Governor still breathes hell-fire, just as he used to,
but something's wrong; no one seems to get punished,
not in the end, not so it hurts.
Do you think the Governor is falling off?
I tell you, a man must live by faith in this colony!

SERGEANT

Don't worry about the Governor's faith.
He's a man much like me, only educated.
You find you can't go on soldiering without
     believing something.
These things are over your head, Soldier;
running a colony takes a lot of juggling.

SOLDIER

What are we doing here?

SERGEANT

This is a war game, Soldier.

> [*More shots are heard off-stage. The* REVELLERS, *terrified and
> with torn clothes, are herded in by* PURITAN SOLDIERS. GOVERNOR
> ENDECOTT *comes last. He is a stern, resolute man with a grizzled
> beard that covers the upper part of his burnished breastplate.*

22

Endecott & the Red Cross

He is followed by a SOLDIER *carrying the Red Cross of England. The* SOLDIERS *ground their matchlock butts on the stage and form into files*]

ENDECOTT

Men, I congratulate you:
on the march from Salem to here, you've kept step like
Spaniards,
you've moved as fast as cavalry.
There's not much here for you,
just a mob of vicious men and women,
dressed up like Hallowe'en children.
Putting them down will be child's-play for you,
but I want you to show that we are humble,
show that we are obedient, show that we are mighty.
We've borne the Red Cross of England to Merry Mount.

SERGEANT

[*Pointing to the Red Cross flag over the doorway*]

Here's another just like it, your Excellency.

ENDECOTT

There are flags and flags.
This one at Merry Mount sags pretty badly,
it bulges in the belly.
I wish these people had had a little fight in them,
then we could have shown them how we handle
    our weapons.
Lead them before me.
I am the arm of God here, Sergeant.

SERGEANT

Here's a fellow gotten up like a wolf, Sir.

23

MAN WITH A WOLF'S HEAD

Spare me, your Excellency!
I put on this wolf's head to amuse my friends.
I was playing the wolf in the fables.

ENDECOTT

This is no wolf! If he were a real wolf,
I'd drive a spike through his tongue and brain,
and hang him to that door till his blood spilled down
    the steps.
This fellow is an old ewe pretending he's a wolf.
We'll stick him in the pillory.
He can howl and grin there 'til sunset.

[*A pillory is brought out.* THE MAN WITH A WOLF'S HEAD *is put in it*]

SERGEANT

Here's a fellow gotten up as a stag, Sir.
What shall we do with him?

MAN WITH A STAG'S HEAD

Spare me, your Excellency!
I am a Christmas reindeer.

ENDECOTT

I see two or three more reindeer behind you.
Put halters on them all and break them in like horses,
Sergeant. They're used to bringing cheer,
they can drag my gun-carriage.

[*Halters are put on the* STAG-MEN. *They draw a cannon across the stage*]
[*An old Puritan elder,* MR. PALFREY, *stumbles on stage. He wears a black cloak and band, a high-crowned hat, and under*]

24

it, a velvet skull-cap. He is out of breath, and his shoes are bemired]

ENDECOTT

Welcome back to us, Elder Palfrey.
I thought you had deserted me for Governor Winthrop
   of Boston.

ELDER PALFREY

Mr. Winthrop is a strict man, your Excellency,
a considering man, but after I'd ministered to him,
I felt homesick for Salem; I said,
there's no one like Endecott.
Endecott knows how to act.
When I heard about this expedition,
the spirit of the Lord descended on me,
my feet hardly touched the ground,
my shoes had wings.
I'm here to help you on this angry day.

ENDECOTT

I need your angry voice, Elder. Up till now,
our demonstration needed salt,
but I am afraid you'll find this day an anti-climax.
I need something stronger to sink my teeth into:
this is routine civilian work.

ELDER PALFREY

Everything you do is the work of God, Sir.

ENDECOTT

I have grown much like Governor Winthrop;
administration has loaded me with *buts* and *ifs*
         and *perhapses*

I go to sleep on duty.
My armor is too heavy. All my joints ache.

ELDER PALFREY

You are a sleeping lion, Sir.

SERGEANT

Here's a young man gotten up like an old witch,
your Excellency. What shall we do with him?

MAN DRESSED UP AS A WITCH

[*In an old woman's falsetto*]

I am anointed with the juice of smallage,
cinque-foil, wolf's bane, and the fat of a new-born babe.

ELDER PALFREY

I know this babbler, your Excellency.
He is as blasphemous here as he was in Boston.
Jam a cleft stick on his tongue
and let it stay there till his tongue drops off!

ENDECOTT

The man of God has spoken, Sergeant.
Fasten a stick to this fellow's tongue
and let him munch on it till sunset.

[*A stick is put in the* YOUNG MAN'S *mouth*]

SERGEANT

Here's an Indian girl, your Excellency.
We caught her dancing with the English people.
She doesn't know a word of English.

ENDECOTT

God be praised, I won't have to listen to her!

26

I thought she was going to tell me she was the children's dancing teacher.

ELDER PALFREY

She may know no English,
but she knows Englishmen well enough;
she is a whore. Heat up a poker, Sergeant,
burn a red *A* on her red cheeks!
This isn't the Church of England that blesses
    such abominations!

ENDECOTT

The man of God has spoken, Sergeant.
Bring out an apron with an *A* sewn on it,
and hang it around the girl's neck.

> [*An apron is put on the* INDIAN GIRL. *From off-stage, an arrow hits* ENDECOTT'S *breast-plate and falls at his feet. He breaks it contemptuously and kicks away the pieces with his armored feet*]

This is like David coming out for Goliath with a sling-shot,
only with far different results. These arrows are toys,
they pop like shuttlecocks off our steel caps
and iron breast-plates. I feel ridiculous
standing here enclosed in iron. I am a mighty fortress.

ELDER PALFREY

They may seem like toys to you, Sir,
but these arrows have killed English women and children;
they have even caught our full-grown men off guard.
There are three thousand miles of wilderness
behind these Indians, enough solid land
to drown the sea from here to England.

We must free our land of strangers,
even if each mile is a marsh of blood!

ENDECOTT

Oh, there's little hope of that, Elder,
the Indians will never make a stand against us.
God help me, there's hardly a day of real soldiering
in a year of Indian fighting.
Here, Sergeant, take six men and round up the Indians.

[THE SOLDIERS *march off.* PALFREY *and* ENDECOTT *come Down Front. The lights begin to darken*]

I feel I am walking in my sleep and in darkness.
I am carrying too much armor. My bones ache.

ELDER PALFREY

I am a much older and weaker man than you are,
your Excellency, but nothing holds me back
when the Lord's work is waiting. On a day like this,
I am a boy of seventeen.
Why do you water down my punishments,
this is no time for gentleness!

ENDECOTT

Have you ever seen a suit of empty armor walking?

ELDER PALFREY

I've never seen one nor hope to;
that's Papist rubbish. It's unchristian of you,
Sir, to wander so and not answer my question.
Why have you watered down my punishments?

ENDECOTT

I am that suit of empty armor.

ELDER PALFREY

Please come back to me, Sir!

ENDECOTT

I have had the fevers lately,
I have been thinking a lot about my wife.
She used to enjoy maskers like these in England.

ELDER PALFREY

God giveth, and God taketh away;
God be praised.

ENDECOTT

I've heard something of the sort,
but never so tersely expressed, Elder.
Come! We are old comrades. I want to speak to you
honestly.
I have been having the fevers. In my fever,
I have been thinking and thinking, as if I paced a
   strange land.

ELDER PALFREY

It's dangerous to think too much on our own,
my old friend. When I am perplexed,
I make my mind a blank and read the Bible.
Then the Lord fills my emptiness with wisdom.

ENDECOTT

I know, Elder. I am familiar with your sermons.
But, you see, in my fever I have had to ask
myself untimely questions, ones I'd never answered.
When my wife died, I went into the army,

as you know. I soon found I couldn't go on fighting
without an iron religion.
I found our iron religion.

ELDER PALFREY

The Lord raised you up.

ENDECOTT

Yes, He certainly raised me up:
Then I came here.
You must bear with me, I am going to give you
a little lesson in statecraft.
When I came here, I found my training
had prepared me to be the Colony policeman.
It was peacetime policework,
not the sort of thing a soldier could take much pride in.
At first my administration was rough and straightforward,
more than Englishmen are used to,
but no more than a frontier religious colony demands.

ELDER PALFREY

You were God's servant who knew how to act.

ENDECOTT

Yes, but it took a lot of thinking,
I found, to work with the government of King Charles.
Each action I took had to be thought of
in the light of the report I could make home on it.
Influential people in England had to be persuaded
        and bribed.
Letters had to be written that would please the King.
and yet allow me leeway to rule in a way

30

that was of course very different from the King's wishes.
I learned to procrastinate and wait on Providence.

ELDER PALFREY

Statecraft is quite over my head, your Excellency.

ENDECOTT

Yes, it's quite unlike the clear,
invigorating air of your pulpit, Elder.
I found there were ways of shouting and lifting my
    armored hand,
and then letting it drop without drawing blood.
I found ways of letting sinners slip through my fingers.
I found I was becoming like myself in the old days,
when I was a worldling and a courtier of King James,
and wooing my wife.

ELDER PALFREY

I will pray for you.

ENDECOTT

No, you haven't heard my story.
I was in this frame of mind, when I fell into a
    chronic fever,
enough to dizzy me, not enough to keep me
    from marching.
I began to see that men are twisted,
that bearing with diseases is the body's business.
I saw that nothing is as clear,
as King Charles and Archbishop Laud and Calvin believe.

ELDER PALFREY

God forbid that you believe
what King Charles and Archbishop Laud believe!

31

ENDECOTT

Ah, but you see, you do believe what they believe:
you are an axe. You are a natural divider.
The whole world sees itself as fuel for a system.
The Catholic Church, Calvin's church,
The State Church of England, the State Church
     of Germany,
divine right kings, imitation Roman republics of fanatics—
A hundred flags and all made of cloth:
he who is not with me is against me.

ELDER PALFREY

You are quoting Scripture.

ENDECOTT

Yes. You will say like the Devil,
but I am talking about my fever.
I had a dream last night. It will interest you.
You are in it, Elder Palfrey.
It has a pastoral simplicity. You know, when I woke up,
it was as though a draft of fresh blue air had blown
through my feverish house which was burning down.

ELDER PALFREY

This is a prophecy of the burning of Merry Mount.

ENDECOTT

No, I am talking about waking from my dream.
In my dream I was you, Elder Palfrey.
I was preaching from your pulpit in Salem,
only I was a grander, more cultured man,
more like the Grand Inquisitor of Spain.
I was wearing black horn-rimmed glasses without lenses,

and read from a black book whose print I couldn't see.
Behind me sat an old man—
I think he was God Almighty;
but he looked like a dirty old Italian Pope,
a yellow slop like cornmeal oozed from a corner of
   his mouth.
Each time I read a sentence, his ringed finger
dropped trembling on my shoulder.
I shivered with fever and rapture.

ELDER PALFREY

You have been mortally sick;
thank God, this was a dream!

ENDECOTT

Each time I read a sentence,
I was sentencing a man to death!
At first, the people weren't people but bits of our black
cloth, or dead leaves tossing in the heat,
or burning off in heaps on the horizon.
The leaves were people somehow. Things grew clearer.
I saw the people of Boston and Salem,
coming before me, one by one:
Winthrops, Dudleys, Williamses, Welds and Peterses.
I was sending them off to be burned,
to an auto-da-fe, as they say on the Continent.
I patted them on the back, kissed them,
told them I knew their sorrows—
my heart was really burning for them.
These people burned like birch logs;
I knew all their names I could see the insides of
   their houses.

33

ELDER PALFREY

Good and evil are all one in dreams, your Excellency.

ENDECOTT

In the end, my own soldiers
were dragging each other to the stake.
I saw their armor melting like lead into the fire.

ELDER PALFREY

Let us kneel together and pray.

ENDECOTT

In the end, I was the only man in the world,
I was alone, and I wasn't even myself.
I was you, Elder, or some other preacher.
I felt my heart oozing through my ribs
like the brown juice of a crushed grasshopper.

ELDER PALFREY

I beg you.
Let us kneel together and pray.

ENDECOTT

[*Still standing*]

I now understand statecraft:
a statesman can either work with merciless efficiency,
and leave a desert,
or he can work in a hit and miss fashion,
and leave a cess-pool.

ELDER PALFREY

Kneel down!

[*They kneel*]

34

ENDECOTT

All men shall surely die, my God,
but You live forever.

[*Pause*]

My mind is clear now. Let me go on with the facts
    of ruling.
I don't believe in dreams any more than you do.
Things here aren't really bad yet,
the King hasn't settled on his course of action;
we can still delay, evade, pull strings.

ELDER PALFREY

You are talking statecraft. This is over my head!

ENDECOTT

Things aren't really bad,
but the time will come, the time will surely come,
I know the King's mind, or rather the minds of
    his advisors—
kings can't be said to have minds.
The rulers of England will revoke our charter,
they will send us a royal Governor,
they will quarter soldiers on us,
they will impose their system of bishops.

ELDER PALFREY

This is a worse nightmare than your dream.
The King will never presume to revoke our charter.

ENDECOTT

Of course the rulers of England will presume,
they wouldn't presume to do anything else but destroy
    us now.

They have been perfecting their plans for ten years.
Their axe is in their hands. We will be abolished.

ELDER PALFREY

Oh, God have mercy on us!
All our saints, all our martyrs,
and all our labors here will perish!
What will we do? What will we do?

ENDECOTT

What will *I* do, you mean.
I will do nothing. I will cave in,
but not for long.
You see, I am only a man of action and active belief.
I am only alive when I am fighting for my life and my faith.
I detest this, but it is so.
I will make a violent speech to my men.
I will say ugly things about the Stuarts,
I will smear the Pope,
I will talk about our liberty of worship,
I will say we have given up everything to live here,
I will ask my soldiers to lay down their lives,
and I will crown my speech with some outrageous act
that will mean that there's no turning back for us,
that England will no longer exist for us.

ELDER PALFREY

That will be a noble speech.

ENDECOTT

No, it turns my stomach.
It will be a hollow, dishonest harangue,
half truth, half bombast—

Let's hope my speech will be practical.
It must stir my soldiers and preachers to fury,
then there will be no toleration, no quarter,
everything here will be Bible, blood and iron.
England will no longer exist.

ELDER PALFREY

I don't understand what you mean by "England will
    not exist."
Will our new commonwealth still exist?—

ENDECOTT

Only God goes on existing. We'll be over quickly.
The King will come and crush us.
The French will move in from the north,
the Dutch will move in from the south.
We won't last,
but we will have our moment,
I will have my hour of exultation and anguish.

[*The stage lightens. The* SOLDIERS *are heard returning*]

ELDER PALFREY

Our soldiers are coming back.
You are tired, your Excellency.
Shall I speak for you and judge the prisoners?

ENDECOTT

You can announce any judgments you like.
I will stand behind you,
and qualify your judgments according to the dictates
of my high office and prudence.

[*The* SERGEANT *and* SOLDIERS *march back on the stage, dragging* THREE *hysterical and drunken* INDIANS. *A* SOLDIER *holds three*

37

broken bows. PALFREY *and* ENDECOTT *walk back and look at the* SOLDIERS]

SERGEANT

I threw three men out in front to make a noisy show,
then marched my three others around the Indians' flank.
Maurice of Nassau's trick. I caught the Indians in a vise.
What shall we do with them, your Excellency?

ENDECOTT

Take over, Elder. We will have
an exhibition of theocracy in action.

ELDER PALFREY

Take the Indians out of sight
and shoot them. This plague must be smothered
if we want our children to live in freedom.

ENDECOTT

The man of God has spoken;
take the Indians out of sight!
There's an ice-house in this settlement, isn't there?
Throw the Indians in the ice-house,
and let them sober up on the saw-dust!

[*A* BEAR *in pink stockings comes out. He dances and paws the air absurdly in front of* ENDICOTT *and* PALFREY]

SERGEANT

Here is the May-King, Sir.
He is young and shining. What shall I do with him?

ELDER PALFREY

Strap the King to a whipping-post,

38

and give him twice as many lashes as the others.
His high station should set an example.

EDWARD

Speak like a Christian, Elder.
If my hands were free, I'd fight you off till you killed me;
since my hands are tied, I won't fight back.
I don't ask mercy for myself,
but pray you not to touch my bride.
We were just married.

ELDER PALFREY

We'll give her something to remember her wedding day by!
We're not in the habit of wasting idle courtesies on women.
We're twice as strict with women.
Sergeant, tie the King and Queen to a whipping-post!

ENDECOTT

Slowly, Elder Palfrey, slowly!
This girl reminds me of my wife.

[*He puts his hand on* EDITH's *shoulder*]

How beautiful you are!

EDITH

Is your wife in Salem, Governor Endecott?
She should see us and soften your judgment on us.

ENDECOTT

What would my wife be doing in Salem?
She was a lovely and intelligent lady.
My wife died twenty-five years ago;
our child died with her.

39

EDITH

So, you became a great Puritan?

ENDECOTT

I became a Puritan.
I believe I am asking the questions, young lady.

[*Puts his hand on* EDITH *again*]

You are almost as beautiful as my wife.
Misfortune has fallen too early on you and your husband.
You will have time to mend. Your husband looks
as if he could handle a matchlock in our militia.
You will come to Salem. You will probably bear children.
I hope they will live.

[*Walks slowly away, as if dreaming, then turns, picks up a
large rose garland and lays it over the heads of* EDWARD *and*
EDITH]
[*Pauses. Then, in a loud voice*]

Sergeant, disrobe the King and Queen,
and give them something practical to wear!

ELDER PALFREY

Shouldn't the King's curled hair be cropped?

ENDECOTT

The voice of divine inspiration has spoken.
Sergeant, cut the King's hair off
in our attractive pumpkin-shell style!

[EDITH *and* EDWARD *are led off*]

40

ELDER PALFREY

[*Angrily*]

Your Excellency!

ENDECOTT

What was I to do, Elder?—
they are children.

ELDER PALFREY

Cleopatra was a child.
I know all I want to about such children.
Remember Michael Wigglesworth's lines on
    unbaptised children?
These are much worse than unbaptised.

[*Sings in a nasal voice*]

Then to the bar they all drew near
Who'd died in infancy;
They never had or good or bad
Effected pers'nally,
But from the womb into the tomb
Had dropped like rotten seed.
They thus began to plead:
"We died before we had transgressed,

If for our own transgressi-on,
Or disobedience,
We here must stand on your right hand,
Just were the recompense;
But Adam's guilt our souls has spilt,
His fault is charged upon us,
And that alone has overthrown
Our spirit and undone us."

Then God replied, "You sinners are,
And sinners shall expect
Such as they'll get, for I do save
None but my own elect."

[*A great sound of shouting.* MORTON *and* MR. BLACKSTONE *walk on stage, followed by two angry* PURITAN SOLDIERS]

MORTON

Very edifying verses, Elder.
I don't know which to admire the more,
their art or their morality. I am a poet myself.

ELDER PALFREY

I know about your poetry. You'll wish you'd stuck
    to poetry,
when we crop your ears, and bore your nose,
and burn down your houses!

MORTON

You ought to be in a strait jacket,
you homicidal Bible-mangling donkey!
I am here to address his Excellency,
John Endecott of Salem.

SOLDIER

We found Morton sitting behind a tree;
he had a gun on his knees,
he was afraid to use it.

MORTON

Everyone in this colony knows, your Excellency,
that I can shoot the head off a grouse at fifty yards.

I could have shot you down quite easily
any time in the last half hour,
but it's against my principles to shed English blood!

ELDER PALFREY

Brand his tongue!

ENDECOTT

No, let him talk.
He is apparently a man of honor,
he tells us I owe my life to his principles.

MORTON

Governor Endecott,
We are both Englishmen. We are both men of culture.
We have both carried the Red Cross of England against
    the Spaniard.
I call on you to treat us with courtesy,
and to allow us our legal rights.

ENDECOTT

This is the first time I've heard of your campaigning,
    Mr. Morton.
I am suppressing you for selling guns and liquor to
    the Indians.
Your Indians are attacking my settlement.

MORTON

You are jealous of our fur trade.
Touch a Puritan's purse, and you'll find a wolf!
I imagine your own men are selling guns to the Indians
whenever your head's turned.
You know how hard it is to keep order on a frontier.

43

ENDECOTT

I have no difficulty keeping order on a frontier,
Mr. Morton. If one of my men dared sell guns to
     the Indians,
he would be put in the stocks and shipped back to England.
We know perfectly well that your men
are selling the Indians guns with your permission.

MORTON

This is a legal question, Mr. Endecott.
The courts in England will settle it.
I am a lawyer myself, I have good lawyers in my pay.
You'll make little headway in England.
It'll be my word against your word, my witnesses against
     your witnesses.
Of course, I know why you hate me,
you hate me for belonging to the Church of England,
and for using the Book of Common Prayer.
I love that book . . .

ENDECOTT

Mr. Morton,
your church and reading habits are neither here nor there.
I am here to enforce moral decorum.
Your May Days are a horror,
your diseased men drink themselves insensible
and live with Indian women.

MORTON

Our May Days are lovely and human,
they are a beautiful old English custom
practiced by your ancestors and mine, Mr. Endecott.

You Puritans walk in blinders.
You look neither to the right nor to the left.
You are only interested in trade.
You beat up my Indians because
they sell me the furs they refuse to sell you . . .

ENDECOTT

This is getting nowhere, Mr. Morton.
I will have to have you gagged.

MORTON

You know, I don't think you will have me tied or gagged,
I have been calling you "Governor" for courtesy,
but you really are no longer a governor.
Your name is Littleworth, not Endecott.
I have a joker up my sleeve here,
if his reverence will excuse me.
This is Mr. Blackstone of the Church of England,
he has a message for you from King Charles.
Speak, Mr. Blackstone, for our church and our King!

MR. BLACKSTONE

Are you Mr. Endecott?

ENDECOTT

I am Endecott.

MR. BLACKSTONE

Mr. Endecott, I am a personal friend of Archbishop Laud.
I have had audiences with King Charles.
I am their emissary.
I hope you will realize that you are no longer talking to

Mr. Morton.
In England, we have a systematic and dignified way
of dealing with you Puritan squires.

ELDER PALFREY

He is a man who cannot bear even the corrupt rule
of his own corrupt church!
He has come to preach evil in the wilderness,
he crowned the May King and Queen!

ENDECOTT

Let him talk, Elder,
he told us he was a systematic and dignified man.

MR. BLACKSTONE

Please attend me, Mr. Endecott.
Do you recognize that flag above our doorway?

ENDECOTT

I see the flag.

MR. BLACKSTONE

I asked you if you recognized the flag of England!

ENDECOTT

I recognize the flag of England.

MR. BLACKSTONE

I represent the flag of England in America.
In the King's name I tell you that the King
has appointed a tribunal for New England,
the head of the tribunal is Archbishop Laud.
Do you know Archbishop Laud, Mr. Endecott?

ELDER PALFREY

Laud is a priest of Baal!

ENDECOTT

You must excuse the elder, Mr. Blackstone,
he is religious.
I know Archbishop Laud,
though I'm afraid I haven't the advantage of his
    personal friendship.

MR. BLACKSTONE

The tribunal for New England
has appointed a Royal Governor;
the Royal Governor will be Sir Ferdinando Gorges.
Do you know Sir Ferdinando Gorges, Mr. Endecott?

ELDER PALFREY

Sir Ferdinando Gorges is our arch-oppressor.
He tried to destroy our colony before we existed!

ENDECOTT

I know Sir Ferdinando, Mr. Blackstone.
We were young men at the court of King James together.
We have had legal disputes for twenty years. I think.

MORTON

I imagine you know then, Endecott,
that Sir Ferdinando and I are table companions.
We are like brothers. When he comes here as a
    Royal Governor,
I shall be at his right hand.
You had better win me over, Littleworth;
my policy is to live and let live.
I am slow to anger. You still have time.

MR. BLACKSTONE

Mr. Endecott, do you realize
that your authority and that
of Governor Winthrop of Boston and Governor Bradford
    of Plymouth
will end when Royal Governor Gorges arrives?

ELDER PALFREY

Ask to see this order in writing, your Excellency!
Tell him we will appeal to the courts in England!

ENDECOTT

You are learning statecraft, Elder.
I am afraid this order will be very clear.
And the courts of England! England has caved in on us.
There is no England!

MR. BLACKSTONE

You see how easily I manage them, Morton?
I speak a few authoritative and logical words,
and they collapse. I am glad I have made myself clear
    to you,
Mr. Endecott. Our new methods have worked wonders
    in England.

ENDECOTT

Will the royal bureaucracy be imposed on New England?

MR. BLACKSTONE

You will have an orderly and systematic government,
    Mr. Endecott.

ENDECOTT

Will the discipline and ceremonial
of the Church of England be imposed on New England?

MR. BLACKSTONE

You will be given an aesthetic, rational
and systematic religion, Mr. Endecott.

ENDECOTT

You see, this is the time I told you of, Elder,
we have little to choose between the corruption of Morton,
and the ruthless systematizing of Archbishop Laud.
They will give us no quarter. This is the day of terror!

ELDER PALFREY

God have mercy on us!

ENDECOTT

I will have to speak to my soldiers.

MORTON

Jupiter thunders,
and the Separatists burst asunder!

MR. BLACKSTONE

You see how our new method works!

> [ENDECOTT *walks slowly over to the house, climbs the steps,*
> *then straightens and turns to the* SOLDIERS]

ENDECOTT

Sergeant, have my men form a line.

SERGEANT

Form a line, Soldiers.

ENDECOTT

Have my men ground arms and stand at attention!

SERGEANT

Ground arms! Attention!

49

ENDECOTT

Sergeant, order the drummers to beat their drums!

SERGEANT

Drummers, beat your drums!

ENDECOTT

Elder, this is a calamitous moment for us.
Give us a brief prayer.

ELDER PALFREY

May God guard and guide our Governor
in all his actions!

ENDECOTT

Soldiers—or must I call you exiles,
now that we have left England?—
Up till now we have acted without words,
and we have been more than adequate for all our dangers.
This is the day of terror!
I want you to think of the country we left.

SOLDIERS

England! England!

ENDECOTT

England, a fine country as countries go,
and probably better than any other in Europe.
The Saxons gave us manpower, the Normans gave us
    a brain.
We have often broken the Scots and occupied
    their kingdom,
We have often broken the French and occupied
    their kingdom.

We have even survived a hundred years of our own
    civil wars.
These wars were prettily called the Wars of the Roses—
they were without decency or grace,
the opposing leaders were as alike as weeds,
men fought for no cause that is intelligible to us now.
When an army lost a battle, it was murdered on the field.
All that's done for, there's no more aristocratic anarchy.
We have shaken off
the foreign, greedy and superstitious Roman Pope;
we have smashed the Spanish fleets.
For over a century and a half, our country has suffered no
    civil disturbance.

MORTON

This is a history lesson, Mr. Endecott!

ENDECOTT

Soldiers, think of the country we left.
It is crowded and complicated,
everything time and tradition could give a country
    is there.
We learned its customs in order to exist,
our ancestors were born and died there,
our kinsmen still live there,
my own wife and child are buried there.
Like many of you, I have served three sovereigns,
I have carried our flag, the Red Cross of England,
against the Spaniard and Rochelle.

SOLDIERS

England! England!

MORTON

This is well spoken, Mr. Endecott.

ENDECOTT

I imagine that my love and service for England
can withstand even your approbation, Mr. Morton.
Soldiers, I ask you, why did I leave England?
Surely, it wasn't disappointment;
I was well spoken of, sought after,
and incessantly employed in court and field.
You, too, according to your conditions,
were men of standing in your towns.
You had cottages and fields.
I had an old stone house with servants.
Why did I come to this waste of animals, Indians and
    nine-month winters?
To this place that has the beauties of nature,
if any care for them, but no civilized substance to it?
Boulders and tree-roots have broken our plow-shares,
our children have cried for bread,
we have torn mussels from the rocks to fill them.
Why did we come here?

MORTON

If the King and Archbishop could hear you,
they would be taking the first ship for Salem,
Freedom for their worship is all they ask for.

ENDECOTT

If you interrupt me again, Mr. Morton,
I'll hang you by your heels to your Maypole,
or perhaps by your neck!

52

Soldiers, as I was saying,
we have given up everything,
we have come here to make a new world for ourselves.
I might almost say,
we have painfully cleared the path to heaven.
Shall Charles Stuart stop us?
Charles is a Scotchman and a pin-headed tailor's model.
His father was James. He slobbered,
he liked to have young boys about him.
James' mother was Mary.
Mary was a whore, a Papist and a criminal murderess,
who blew her husband up with powder.
Her death at the block shows us perhaps
what divinity guards her grandson's crown.

MR. BLACKSTONE

This is treason, Mr. Endecott!
You will be sent to the Tower. You will be beheaded.

ENDECOTT

I am talking about the future, Mr. Blackstone.
Soldiers, Charles Stuart is going to hand us over to Laud,
Old Thorough, our most logical persecutor.
King and Bishop are taking counsel together.
They have appointed a governor-general,
the governor-general is going to establish the corrupt
    Church of England here;
there will be a bishop in every county,
a priest in every parish.

SOLDIERS

God save us from King Charles!

ENDECOTT

If the King and Bishop have their way,
there will be a cross and high altar in every meeting-house,
a royal official in every court,
you will serve under good-for-nothing
      gentleman lieutenants.
Candles will burn at noonday even on the steps to
      the pulpit.
Will you wait for this without drawing a sword,
without firing a gun, without spilling blood?

SOLDIERS

God save us!

ENDECOTT

No! We shall make a stand in this land,
we shall stand on this land,
that we have brought our possessions to,
that we have cleared with our axes,
that we have broken with our plows,
that we have pacified with our guns,
that we have sanctified with our prayers.
God brought us here, shall man enslave us?
What have we to do with mitred bishops?
What have we to do with anointed kings?
What have we to do with England?

SOLDIERS

What have we to do with England?

ENDECOTT

Bring me our standard,
the Red Cross of England!

SERGEANT

Yes, Sir.

ENDECOTT

Sergeant, tear the Red Cross from its staff!

SERGEANT

I am afraid to. I am a soldier;
I served against Spain under this flag.

ENDECOTT

It's nothing.

> [*Draws his sword and cuts the Red Cross from its staff. It falls to the ground at his feet*]

Before God and man, I stand by my act!
We shall have no pope or tyrant or mother-country in
    New England!
No flag shall stand between us and our God!

SOLDIERS

No flag shall stand between us and our God!

> [*They cheer* ENDECOTT. *Drums are beaten*]

MR. BLACKSTONE

This is treason and blasphemy!

ENDECOTT

Sergeant, tie up Mr. Blackstone.
Morton is quiet at last, but you'd better tie him up, too.

SERGEANT

Yes, Sir.

ENDECOTT

Sergeant, take these people of Merry Mount away.

[*Pauses*]

Wait a minute. I have a fancy, Sergeant.
Let them perform their more decorous masque for the
    last time.

[*The* REVELLERS *dance the stately sedate dance they danced previously. Their manner is quite changed, they perform pathetically and wiltingly*]

REVELLERS

Fair and fair, and twice so fair,
as fair as any may be,
the fairest shepherd on our green,
a love for any lady.

[EDWARD *and* EDITH *lead the dance. He is now in gray clothes and has cropped hair.* EDITH *is also dressed in gray*]

Fair and fair, and twice so fair,
listen to Cupid's curse:
all they who change old love for new,
pray God they change for worse.

ENDECOTT

This is the last masque that will be heard in New England.
Sergeant, take these people away!

SERGEANT

Yes, Sir.

ENDECOTT

Then go to the ice-house and release the Indians.
Take them out in a field and shoot them!

SERGEANT

Yes, Sir.

ENDECOTT

Sergeant, when our men are finished with the Indians,
they can start burning down the houses of Merry Mount.

SERGEANT

Yes, Sir.

ENDECOTT

Tomorrow, we will burn the Indian village.

SERGEANT

Yes, Sir.

[THE SOLDIERS, *with* THE REVELLERS, *leave.* ENDECOTT *stands
alone, brooding.* ELDER PALFREY *comes up to him*]

ENDECOTT

You see, I've made my speech and performed my act.
The earth hasn't swallowed us.

ELDER PALFREY

It was the finest speech I've ever heard outside the pulpit,
your Excellency.

ENDECOTT

No, I don't suppose so,
I wasn't really listening.
These maskers make me think of my youth in England.

57

ELDER PALFREY

Don't look backward. Remember how Lot's wife
was turned into a pillar of salt for looking backward.

ENDECOTT

Oh, stop it, Elder!
you need a rest.
Go out and watch the Indians die:
they deserve the blessing of your presence.

ELDER PALFREY

Yes, your Excellency.

[*As* ELDER PALFREY *leaves,* THE SERGEANT *comes running on*]

SERGEANT

You have given no orders for our treatment of the
        Merry Mount people.
Shall I double their punishments?

ENDECOTT

No, I don't think so.
We are burning down their houses.
I'll do something tomorrow,
or the next day.
I will delay and wait on Providence.

SERGEANT

Yes, Sir.

> [*He leaves the stage*]
> [ENDECOTT *remains alone for a few moments, head down and
> brooding. He lifts the fallen Red Cross of England with his
> foot*]

58

ENDECOTT

It's strange I was in such an unmanly terror about a flag.

[*Pause. He kicks the flag off the steps*]

It's a childish thing.

CURTAIN

MY KINSMAN,
MAJOR MOLINEUX

ORIGINAL CAST FOR

My Kinsman, Major Molineux
Premiere November 1, 1964, American Place Theatre

Robin: THOMAS J. STUBBLEFIELD

Boy (his brother): BLAISE MORTON

Ferryman: CLAYTON CORBIN

1st Redcoat: WILLIAM JACOBSON

2nd Redcoat: ROBERT TINSLEY

First Barber: JAY DOYLE

Tavern Keeper: LOGAN RAMSEY

Man with Pewter Mug: JAMES ZAFERES

Clergyman: THOMAS BARBOUR

Prostitute: SCOTTIE MACGREGOR

Colonel Greenough: TOM MCDERMOTT

Man in Periwig: HEYWOOD HALE BROUN

Watchman: JACK RYLAND

Major Molineux: GAYLORD C. MASON

Citizens of Boston: HOWARD MARTIN, LUKE ANDREAS,
   CONWAY W. YOUNG, RICHARD KJELLAND,
   SIGRUNN WAAGE, ANTONIE BECKER,
   E. EMMET WALSCH, MARTHA NEAG,
   JAMES ZAFERES, JILL MALIN, PAUL PLUMMER

The scene

Boston, just before the American Revolution. *Date changed 4-1734*

To the left of the stage, ROBIN, a young man barely eighteen, in a coarse grey coat, well-worn but carefully repaired, leather breeches, blue yarn stockings, and a worn three-cornered hat. He carries a heavy oak-sapling cudgel and has a wallet slung over his shoulder. Beside him, his brother, a BOY of ten or twelve, dressed in the same respectable but somewhat rustic manner. On the far left of the stage, the triangular prow of a dory; beside it, a huge FERRYMAN holding an upright oar. He has a white curling beard. His dress, although eighteenth century, half suggests that he is Charon. Lined across the stage and in the style of a primitive New England sampler, are dimly seen five miniature houses: a barber shop, a tavern, a white church, a shabby brick house with a glass bay window, and a pillared mansion, an official's house, on its cornice the golden lion and unicorn of England. The houses are miniature, but their doors are man-size. Only ROBIN, his BROTHER, and the FERRYMAN are lit up.

ROBIN

Here's my last crown, your double price
for ferrying us across the marsh
at this ungodly hour.

FERRYMAN

A crown!

Do you want me to lose my soul?
Do you see King George's face?
judging us on this silver coin?
I have no price.

ROBIN

You asked for double.

FERRYMAN

I'll take the crown for your return trip.

[*Takes the coin*]

No one returns.

ROBIN

No one?

FERRYMAN

No one.
Legs go round in circles here.
This is the city of the dead.

ROBIN

What's that?

FERRYMAN

I said this city's Boston,
No one begs here. Are you deaf?

[*The little houses on stage light up, then dim out*]

ROBIN

[*To the* FERRYMAN]

Show me my kinsman's mansion. You

66

must know him—Major Molineux,
the most important man in town.

FERRYMAN

The name's familiar . . . Molineux . . .
Wasn't he mixed up with the French?
He's never at home now. If you'll wait
here, you'll meet him on his rounds.
All our important people drift
sooner or later to my ferry landing,
and stand here begging for the moon.
You'll see your cousin. You're well-placed.

ROBIN

I know it. My kinsman's a big man here.
He told me he would make my fortune;
I'll be a partner in his firm,
either here or in London.

FERRYMAN

       Settle
for London, that's your city, Boy.
Majors are still sterling silver across
the waters. All the English-born
suddenly seem in love with London.
Your cousin's house here is up for sale.

ROBIN

He cares for England. *Rule Britannia,*
that's the tune he taught me. I'm
surprised he's leaving.

67

FERRYMAN

    He's surprised!
He seemed to belong here once. He wished
to teach us *Rule Britannia,* but
we couldn't get it through our heads.
He gave us this to keep us singing.

    [*The* FERRYMAN *holds up a boiled lobster*]

ROBIN

You're joking, it's a lobster.

FERRYMAN

    No.
Look, it's horny, boiled and red,
It is the Major's spitting image.

    [*On the other side of the stage,* TWO BRITISH REDCOATS *are seen marching slowly in step with shouldered muskets.* Rule Britannia *played faintly*]

FERRYMAN

    [*Pointing to* SOLDIERS]

Here are the Major's chicken lobsters.

ROBIN

Our soldiers!

FERRYMAN

    We call them lobsterbacks.
They are the Major's privates. Wherever
they are gathered together, he is present.
You'll feel his grip behind their claws.

68

What are you going to do now:
run home to Deerfield, take a ship
for England, Boy, or chase the soldiers?

ROBIN

Why, I'm staying here. I like
soldiers. They make me feel at home.
They kept the Frenchmen out of Deerfield.
They'll tell me where my kinsman lives.

FERRYMAN

The French are finished. The British
are the only Frenchmen left.
Didn't you say your cousin's name
was Molineux?

ROBIN

He's Norman Irish.
Why are you leaving?

FERRYMAN

Money. The soldiers
make me pay them for the pleasure
of shuttling them across the marsh.
Run, Boy, and catch those soldiers' scarlet
coat-tails, while they're still around.

[*The* FERRYMAN *goes off pushing his boat*]
[ROBIN *and the* BOY *advance towards the* SOLDIERS]

ROBIN

I need your help, Sirs.

FIRST SOLDIER
[*Smiling*]

We are here
for service, that's our unpleasant duty.

ROBIN

I liked the way
the soldiers smiled. I wonder how
anyone could distrust a soldier.

BOY

We've lost our guide.

ROBIN

We'll find another.

BOY

Why did that boatman gnash his teeth
at Cousin Major?

ROBIN

He was cold.
That's how big city people talk.
Let's walk. We're here to see the city.

[*As* ROBIN *and the* BOY *start moving, the miniature houses light up one by one and then go dark. A* BARBER *comes out of the barber shop; he holds a razor, and a bowl of suds. A* TAVERN KEEPER *enters holding a newspaper*]

BARBER

[*Cutting away the suds with his razor*]

That's how we shave a wig.

70

My Kinsman, Major Molineux

TAVERN KEEPER

        You mean
a Tory.

BARBER

        Shave them to the bone!

TAVERN KEEPER

[*Pointing to newspaper*]

Here's the last picture of King George;
He's passed another tax on tea.

BARBER

Health to the King, health to the King!
Here's rum to drown him in the tea!

[*Drenches the newspaper with his mug*]
[A CLERGYMAN, *white-wigged, all in black, comes out of the church*]

CLERGYMAN

What an ungodly hour! The city's
boiling. All's rum and revolution.
We have an everlasting city,
but here in this unsteady brightness,
nothing's clear, unless the Lord
enlighten us and show the winner!

[*A* PROSTITUTE *comes out of the bay-window house. She wears a red skirt and a low, full-bosomed white blouse*]

PROSTITUTE

Here in the shadow of the church,

71

I save whatever God despises—
Whig or Tory, saint or sinner,
I'm their refuge from the church.

> [*The pillared mansion lights up. A* MAN *comes out in a blue coat and white trousers like General Washington's. He wears a grayish mask covered with pocks. His forehead juts out and divides in a double bulge. His nose is a yellow eagle's beak. His eyes flash like fire in a cave. He looks at himself in a mirror*]

MAN WITH MASK

My mind's on fire. This fire will burn
the pocks and paleness from my face.
Freedom has given me this palace.
I'll go and mingle with the mob.

> [*Now the houses are dark.* ROBIN *rubs his eyes in a daze, stares into the darkness, then turns to his brother*]

BOY

Who are these people, Brother Robin?
We're in the dark and far from Deerfield.

ROBIN

We're in the city, little brother.
Things will go smoother when we find
our kinsman, Major Molineux.

BOY

Our kinsman isn't like these people.
He is a loyal gentleman.

72

My Kinsman, Major Molineux

ROBIN

We'll see. He swore he'd make my fortune,
and teach you Latin.

BOY

I want something.

ROBIN

Let's see the city.

BOY

I want a flintlock.

[*A* MAN *enters from the right. He wears a full gray periwig, a wide-skirted coat of dark cloth and silk stocking rolled up above the knees. He carries a polished cane which he digs angrily into the ground at every step. "Hem, hem," he says in a sepulchral voice as he walks over to the barber shop. The* TWO BARBERS *appear,* ONE *with a razor, the* OTHER *with a bowl of suds*]

MAN IN PERIWIG

Hem! Hem!

ROBIN

Good evening, honored sir.
Help us. We come from out of town.

MAN IN PERIWIG

A good face and a better shoulder!
Hem, hem! I see you're not from Boston.
We need good stock in Boston. You're lucky!
meeting me here was providential.
I'm on the side of youth. Hem, hem!

73

I'll be your guiding lamp in Boston.
Where do you come from?

ROBIN

Deerfield.

MAN IN PERIWIG

Deerfield!
Our bulwark from the savages!
Our martyred village! He's from Deerfield,
Barber. We can use his muscle.

BARBER

You can feel it.

MAN IN PERIWIG

[*Seeing the* BOY]

Look, a child!

BARBER

Shall I shave him?

MAN IN PERIWIG

Yes, shave him.
Shave him and teach him to beat a drum.

BOY

I want a flintlock.

MAN IN PERIWIG

A gun! You scare me!
Come on Apollo, we must march.
We'll put that shoulder to the wheel.
Come, I'll be your host in Boston.

My Kinsman, Major Molineux

ROBIN

I have connections here, a kinsman . . .

MAN IN PERIWIG

Of course you have connections here.
They will latch on to you like fleas.
This is your town! Boy! With that leg
You will find kinsmen on the moon.

ROBIN

My kinsman's Major Molineux.

MAN IN PERIWIG

Your kinsman's Major Molineux!
Let go my coat cuff, Fellow. I have
authority, authority!
Hem! Hem! Respect your betters. Your leg
will be acquainted with the stocks
by peep of day! You fellows help me!
Barber, this man's molesting me!

FIRST BARBER

[Closing in]

Don't hit His Honor, Boy!

SECOND BARBER

His Honor
is a lover of mankind!

BOY

Brain him with your cudgel, Robin!

75

ROBIN

Come, Brother, we will see the city;
they're too many of them and one has a razor.

[ROBIN *and the* BOY *back off. Barber shop goes dark*]

BOY

Who was that fellow, Brother Robin?

ROBIN

He is some snotty, county clerk,
chipping and chirping at his betters.
He isn't worth the Major's spit.

BOY

You should have brained him with your stick.

ROBIN

Let's go, now. We must see the city
and try to find our kinsman's house.
I am beginning to think he's out
of town. Look, these men will help us.

[*The tavern lights up. A sign with King George III's head
hangs in front. There's a poster nailed to the door. The* MAN
WITH THE MASK *strolls over and sits in the chair*]

CROWD

Health to the rattlesnake. A health
to Colonel Greenough! He's our man!

MAN WITH MASK

A shine, men, you must shine my shoes
so bright King George will see his face
flash like a guinea on the toe.

76

My Kinsman, Major Molineux

CROWD

Health to the rattlesnake!

TAVERN KEEPER

[*Turning to* ROBIN]

You boys
are from the country, I presume.
I envy you, you're seeing Boston
for the first time. Fine town, there's lots
to hold you, English monuments,
docks, houses, and a fleet of tea-ships
begging for buyers. I trust you'll stay;
nobody ever leaves this city.

ROBIN

We come from Deerfield.

TAVERN KEEPER

Then you'll stay;
no Indians scalp us in our beds;
our only scalper is this man here.

[*General laughter*]

ROBIN

Our massacre was eighty years
ago. We're not frontiersmen now,
we've other things to talk about.

BARBER

He has other things to talk about.
This boy's a gentleman. He is
no redskin in a coonskin cap.

I'm on our village council. I've
read Plutarch.

TAVERN KEEPER

You are an ancient Roman.
You'll find you like our commonwealth.
I crave the honor of your custom.
I've whiskey, gin and rum and beer,
and a spruce beer for your brother.

BOY

I want a real beer.

BARBER

Give them beer.

[*Shouting*]

TAVERN KEEPER

Two real beers for the Deerfield boys,
they have the fighting Deerfield spirit.

ROBIN

I'm sure you'll trust me for your money.
I have connections here in Boston,
my kinsman's Major Molineux.
I spent our money on this journey.

MAN

His kinsman's Major Molineux;
sometimes a boy is short of money!

[*Laughter*]

MAN

[*Bringing out a silver Liberty Bowl*]

I've something stronger than beer.
Here is the Bowl of Liberty.
The Major dropped this lobster in
the bowl. It spikes the drink.

[MAN *puts down his mug and lifts a lobster out of bowl.*]
[*Cheers*]

ROBIN

I know
the lobster is a British soldier.

MAN

Yes, there they are.

[*The* TWO REDCOATS *march on stage as before. Silence. The* MAN WITH THE MASK *starts writing on a bench. The* SOLDIERS *saunter over to him*]

FIRST SOLDIER

What are you writing, Colonel Greenough?

MAN WITH MASK

My will.

FIRST SOLDIER

Things aren't that desperate.

MAN WITH MASK

I'm adding up my taxes, Redcoat.
Just counting up the figures kills me.
My bankers say I'm burning money.

I can't afford your bed and board
and livery, Soldiers. We'll have to part.

SECOND SOLDIER

I've had enough. We ought to throw
them all in jail.

FIRST SOLDIER

     Go easy.

ROBIN

    [*Walking shyly up to* SOLDIERS]

       Sir,
I need your guidance, I'm looking for
my kinsman, Major Molineux.

FIRST SOLDIER

Watch your words!

SECOND SOLDIER

    Damn your insolence!

FIRST SOLDIER

We'll haul you to the Major's court.

    [*Shots and screams off stage.* SOLDIERS *leave on the run*]

MAN

    [*Pointing to* ROBIN]

He's one of us.

SECOND MAN

    He is a spy.

CROWD

Both boys are spies or Tories.

TAVERN KEEPER

[*Drawing* ROBIN *over to the poster*]

Look,
do you see this poster? It says,
"Indentured servant, Jonah Mudge:
ran from his master's house, blue vest,
oak cudgel, leather pants, small brother,
and his master's third best hat.
Pound sterling's offered any man
who nabs and lodges him in jail."
Trudge off, Young Man, you'd better trudge!

CROWD

Trudge, Jonah Mudge, you'd better trudge!

BOY

They're drunk. You'd better hit them, Robin.

ROBIN

They'd only break my stick and brains.

BOY

For God's sake stand and be a man!

ROBIN

No, they're too many, little brother.
Come, I feel like walking.
We haven't seen the city yet.

[*Lights go off.* ROBIN *and* BOY *stand alone*]

BOY

We haven't seen our kinsman, Robin.
I can't see anything.

ROBIN

You'd think
the Major's name would stand us for
a beer. It's a funny thing, Brother, naming
our kinsman, Major Molineux,
sets all these people screaming murder.
Even the soldiers.

> [*The house with the bay-window lights up. A woman's red skirt and bare shoulders are clearly visible through the window. She is singing*]

WOMAN

Soldiers, sailors.
Whig and Tories, saints and sinners,
I'm your refuge from despair.

ROBIN

[*Knocks*]

Sweet, pretty mistress, help me. I
am tired and lost. I'm looking for
my kinsman, Major Molineux.
You have bright eyes.

WOMAN

I know your kinsman.
Everybody is my kinsman here.

ROBIN

Yes, I am sure. You have kind eyes.
My kinsman is a blood relation.

WOMAN

You're my blood relation too then.
What a fine back and leg you have!
You're made right.

ROBIN

       Oh, I will be made
when I find my kinsman. You
must know him, he's a man of some
importance in your city, Lady.

WOMAN

The Major dwells here.

ROBIN

You're thinking of some other major,
Lady; mine is something more
important than a major, he's
a sort of royal governor,
and a man of fortune. Molineux
tea ships sail from here to China.
He has a gilded carriage, twenty
serving men, two flags of England
flying from his lawn. You could hide
your little house behind a sofa
in his drawing-room.

WOMAN

       I know,

your kinsman is a man of parts,
that's why he likes to camp here. Sometimes
his greatness wearies him. These days
even kings draw in their horns,
and mingle with the common people.
Listen, you'll hear him snoring by
the roof.

ROBIN

                I hear a hollow sound.
My kinsman must be happy here.
I envy him this hideaway.

WOMAN

You mean to say you envy him
the mistress of his house. Don't worry,
a kinsman of the Major's is
my kinsman. I knew you right away.
You have your kinsman's leg and shoulders.
He wears an old three-cornered hat
and leather small-clothes here in the rain.
Why, you *are* the good old gentleman,
only you're young! What is this cloth?
You've good material on your leg.

[*The* WOMAN *feels the cloth of* ROBIN's *trousers*]

ROBIN

It's deerskin. I'm from Deerfield, Lady.

WOMAN

You must be starved. I'll make you happy.

My Kinsman, Major Molineux

ROBIN

I'll wait here on your doorstep, Lady.
Run up and tell the Major that
his Deerfield cousins are in town.

WOMAN

The Major'd kill me, if I woke him.
You see, he spilled a little too much
rum in his tea.

ROBIN

I'll leave a note then. I must go,
my little brother needs some sleep.

[WOMAN *takes* ROBIN's *hat and twirls it on her finger*]

What are you doing with my hat?

WOMAN

I'm showing you our Boston rites
of hospitality. The Major
would kill me, if I turned you out
on such a night. I even have
a downstairs bedroom for your brother.
I find a playroom comes in handy.

BOY

I want to go with Robin.

WOMAN

            Oh, dear,
children keep getting me in trouble.
We have a law.

          [*A bell is heard off stage*]

Mother of God!

[*The* WOMAN *ducks into her house*]
[*Her light goes out*]·

BOY

Why did the lady slam her door?

ROBIN

The bell reminded her of something.
She has to catch up on her sleep.

BOY

Has the Major left his mansion?
Is he really sleeping here?

ROBIN

How can I tell you? Everyone
answers us in riddles.

BOY

        She said,
the Major dwells here.

ROBIN

        That's her city
way of being friendly, Brother.

BOY

Robin, the Major could afford
to buy the lady better clothes.
She was almost naked.

86

ROBIN

>She
was dressed unwisely.

BOY

>Isn't Eve
almost naked in our Bible?

ROBIN

Don't ask so many questions, brother.
I wish I knew the naked truth.

>[*A* WATCHMAN *enters, dishevelled and yawning. He holds a
lantern with a bell tied to it and a spiked staff*]

WATCHMAN

Stop, we don't allow this sort
of talk about the Bible here.

ROBIN

You are mistaken, Sir. I said
I wished I knew the naked truth.

WATCHMAN

You're in New England. Here we fine
mothers for bearing naked children.
You're leading this child into perdition.
We have a fine for that. What's in
your wallet, Boy?

ROBIN

Nothing.

WATCHMAN

>Nothing! You've been inside then!

ROBIN

Watchman, I'm looking for my kinsman.

WATCHMAN

And you thought you'd find him in this house
Doing his martial drill.

ROBIN

       You know him!
My kinsman's Major Molineux.
I see you know him, he will pay you
if you will lead us to his house.

WATCHMAN

   [Singing]

   Your aunt's the lord high sheriff,
   your uncle is King George;
   if you can't pay the tariff,
   the house will let you charge.

ROBIN

I asked for Major Molineux.

WATCHMAN

Keep asking! We are cleaning house.
The Major's lost a lot of money
lately, buying bad real estate.
He can't afford his country cousins.
Move, you filthy, sucking hayseed!
or I'll spike you with my stick!

BOY

Why don't you hit him, brother?

My Kinsman, Major Molineux

WATCHMAN

    I'll have
you in the stocks by daybreak, Boy.

ROBIN

We'll go, Sir. I'm your countryman
learning the customs of the city.

WATCHMAN

    [*Goes off singing*]

> *Baggy buttocks, baggy buttocks,*
> *The Queen of England's willing*
> *To serve you for a shilling*
> *And stick you in the stocks.*

ROBIN

    We're learning
how to live. The man was drunk.

BOY

Our Deerfield watchmen only drink
at Communion. Something's wrong,
these people need new blood.

ROBIN

    Perhaps
they'll get it. Here's a clergyman,
he'll tell us where to find our kinsman.

    [*The* CLERGYMAN *comes across the stage. He is awkwardly holding a large English flag on a staff*]

89

ROBIN

Help me, I beg you, Reverend Sir,
I'm from Deerfield, I'm looking for
my kinsman, Major Molineux.
No one will tell me where he lives.

CLERGYMAN

I have just left the Major's house.
He is my patron and example.
A good man—it's a pity though
he's so outspoken; other good men
misunderstand the Major's meaning.
He just handed me this British
flag to put above my pulpit—
a bit outspoken!

ROBIN

            Our country's flag, Sir!

CLERGYMAN

Yes, a bit outspoken. Come
I'll lead you to your kinsman's house.

> [*The* MAN WITH THE MASK *strides hurriedly across the stage,
> and unrolls a rattlesnake flag, which he hands to the* CLERGY-
> MAN, *who has difficulty in managing the two flags*]

MAN WITH MASK

I have a present for you, Parson:
our Rattlesnake. "Don't tread on me!"
it says. I knew you'd want to have one.
Hang it up somewhere in church;

there's nothing like the Rattlesnake
for raising our declining faith.

CLERGYMAN

I thank you, Sir.

MAN WITH MASK

You'd better hurry.
Think of the man who had no garment
for the wedding. Things are moving.

[MAN WITH MASK *hurries off stage*]

CLERGYMAN

[*To himself*]

God help us, if we lose!

[*Turns to go*]

ROBIN

Sir, you're leaving! You promised me
you'd lead me to my kinsman's house.
Please, let me help you with the flags.

CLERGYMAN

I'll see you later. I have to hurry.
I have a sick parishioner,
a whole sick parish! I have a notion
one of these flags will cure us. Which?
Everyone's so emphatic here.
If you should meet your kinsman, tell him
I'm praying for him in my church.

[CLERGYMAN *goes out*]
[*A loud "hem, hem" is heard. The* MAN IN THE PERIWIG *comes*

jauntily forward followed by the TWO BARBERS. *He goes to the house with the bay-window and raps with his cane. The light inside the house goes on. A rattlesnake flag has been nailed to the door. No one sees* ROBIN *and the* BOY] In course of the pro.

FIRST BARBER

Look, Your Honor, Mrs. Clark
has taken on the Rattlesnake.

MAN IN PERIWIG

Good, this pricks my fainting courage.
"Don't tread on me!" That's rather odd
for Mrs. Clark.

FIRST BARBER

Come on, your Honor.

SECOND BARBER

There's always a first time.

FIRST BARBER

Then a second.

MAN IN PERIWIG

Thank God, I've but one life to give
my country.
Lay on, Macduff! I owe this to
my reputation, boys.

FIRST BARBER

He owes
his reputation to the boys.

92

SECOND BARBER

Between the devil and the deep
blue sea, Your Honor!

FIRST BARBER

His Honor likes
the sea. Everyone loves a sailor.

MAN IN PERIWIG

Hurry! I'm in torture! Open!
I have authority hem, hem!

[MAN IN PERIWIG *knocks loudly. The* WOMAN *stands in door-way*]

WOMAN

[*Singing*]

Where is my boy in leather pants,
who gives a woman what she wants?

MAN IN PERIWIG

[*Singing in falsetto*]

Woman, I have a royal Crown
your countryman gave the ferryman
a-standing on the strand;
but money goes from hand to hand:
the crown is on the town,
the money's mine, I want to dine.
Whatever we do is our affair,
the breath of freedom's in the air.

FIRST BARBER

The lady's ballast's in the air.

Two ten pound tea chests. The lady needs
a little uplift from the clergy.

MAN IN PERIWIG

I'm breaking on the foamy breakers!
Help! help!
I wish my lady had a firm,
hard-chested figure like a mast,
but what has love to do with fact?
A lover loves his nemesis;
the patriotic act.

> [*The* MAN IN THE PERIWIG *gives the lady the crown and passes in. The lights go out*]

BARBER

Once to every man and nation
comes the time a gentleman
wants to clear his reputation.

TAVERN KEEPER

Once to every man and nation
comes the time a man's a man.

BARBER

His Honor's perished on the blast.

> [*The* BARBER *saunters off along with* TAVERN KEEPER. *The* BOY *turns to* ROBIN, *who is lost in thought*]

ROBIN

      I think the Major
has left. By watching I have learned

94

to read the signs. The Rattlesnake
means Major Molineux is out.
A British flag means he's at home.

BOY

You talk in riddles like the town.

ROBIN

Say what you mean; mean what you say:
that's how we used to talk in Deerfield.
It's not so simple here in the city.

> [*The pillared mansion lights up.* ROBIN *and the* BOY *approach
> it. The Lion and Unicorn of England are gone. Instead, a
> large Rattlesnake flag is showing*]

Brother, we've reached our destination.
This is our kinsman's house. I know it
from the steel engraving that
he gave us when he came to Deerfield.
Our journey's over. Here's our mansion.

BOY

Robin, it has a Rattlesnake.

ROBIN

That means the Major's not at home.

> [*The* MAN WITH THE MASK *comes out of the mansion. Half his
> face is now fiery red, the other half is still mottled*]

MAN WITH MASK

I am the man on horseback.

ROBIN

No,
you're walking, Sir.

MAN WITH MASK

I am a king.

ROBIN

The king's in England. You must be sick.
Have you seen your face? Half's red,
the other half is pocked and mottled.

MAN WITH MASK

Oh I'm as healthy as the times.
I am an image of this city.
Do you see this colored handkerchief?

[MAN WITH MASK *draws out a small British flag*]

ROBIN

Our British flag, Sir.

MAN WITH MASK

Yes, it doesn't
help my illness any more,
when I try to cool my burning brow,
or blow my nose on it.

ROBIN

I know
a man who used to own this house.
Let's see if he's still here. Perhaps,
my friend can help to heal your sickness.

MAN WITH MASK

My face will be entirely red soon;
then I'll be well. Who is your friend?

ROBIN

A kinsman, Major Molineux.

MAN WITH MASK

I have a fellow feeling for him.
The Major used to own this house:
now it's mine. I'm taking over,
I've just signed the final deed.
Do you see my nameplate on the gate?

ROBIN

The Rattlesnake?

MAN WITH MASK

      The Rattlesnake.

ROBIN

If I pick up the Rattlesnake,
will it help me find my kinsman?
I think he needs my help. We are
his last relations in the world.

MAN WITH MASK

The last shall be the first, my Boy.

ROBIN

What do you mean? You talk like Christ.

MAN WITH MASK

The first shall be the last, my Boy.

The Major has a heavy hand;
we have been beaten to the ground.

ROBIN

My kinsman has an open hand.

MAN WITH MASK

Ridden like horses, fleeced like sheep,
worked like cattle, clothed and fed
like hounds and hogs!

ROBIN

      I want to find him.

MAN WITH MASK

Whipping-posts, gibbets, bastinadoes
and the rack! I must be moving.

ROBIN

Wait, I'll take up the Rattlesnake.
Please, help me find my kinsman.

    [ROBIN *takes hold of the* MAN WITH THE MASK'S *shoulder. The*
    MAN *steps back and draws his sword*]

MAN WITH MASK

      Move!
You've torn my cloak. You'd better keep
a civil tongue between your teeth.
I have a mission.

    [ROBIN *raises his cudgel. He and the* MAN WITH THE MASK *stand*
    a moment facing each other]

BOY

      Brain him, Robin.

Mangle the bastard's bloody face.
He doesn't like our kinsman, Robin.

ROBIN

I only asked for information.

MAN WITH MASK

For information! Information
is my trade. I was a lawyer
before I learned the pleasures of
the military life. The Major
was my first teacher. Now I know you!
I met you at the tavern. You
were short of cash then. Take this crown:
drink to the Major, then a health
to Greenough, and the Rattlesnake.
To Greenough!

ROBIN

        You're a fighter.

MAN WITH MASK

I hate war, wars leave us where
they find us, don't they, boy
Let's talk about my health.

ROBIN

        Where can
I find my kinsman?

MAN WITH MASK

        He owned this house.
Men used to find him here all day,

99

before the storms disturbed his judgment,
He's out now ranging through the town,
looking for new accommodations.
Wait here. You'll meet him on his walk.

[*Strides off singing*]

The king is in his counting house;
we're counting up his money.

BOY
Why was that fellow's face half red now?
He's changing color.

ROBIN
   I don't know.
He is someone out of "Revelations"—
Hell revolting on its jailers.

[*The church lights up a little.* ROBIN *walks over to it, and*
looks in a window]

Our church is empty, brother. Moonbeams
are trembling on the snow-pure pews,
the altar's drowned in radiant fog,
a single restless ray has crept
across the open Bible.

[*Turns to a gravestone by the church*]

   I'm lonely.
What's this? A gravestone? A grave? Whose grave?
I think the Major must have died:
everything tells me he is gone
and nothing is forever.

My Kinsman, Major Molineux

[*Turns back to the church*]

Brother,
the moon's the only worshipper!

[*The* CLERGYMAN *comes out of the church. He lays a white clay pipe on the steps and holds up a little colored celluloid whirligig*]

CLERGYMAN

The wind has died.

ROBIN

What are you doing?

CLERGYMAN

I'm playing with this whirligig,
and waiting to see which way the wind
will veer. It's quite amusing, Son,
trying to guess the whims of the wind.
I am waiting for a sign.
A strange thing for a modern churchman.

ROBIN

My father says the Church is a rock.

CLERGYMAN

Yes, yes, a rock is blind. That's why
I've shut my eyes.

ROBIN

I see my father. He's the Deerfield
minister, and Church of England.
You remind me of my father.

101

CLERGYMAN

Be careful, son. Call no man father:
that's what we tell the Roman clergy;
sometimes I think we go too far,
they get their people out for Mass.

ROBIN

Father. When I shut
my eyes, I dream I'm back in Deerfield.
The people sit in rows below
the old oak; a horseman stops to water
his horse and to refresh his soul.
I hear my father holding forth
thanksgiving, hope and all the mercies—

CLERGYMAN

Those village
pastors! Once they used to preach
as if the world were everlasting;
each Sunday was longer than a summer!
That's gone now. We have competition:
taverns, papers, politics
and trade. It takes a wolfhound now
to catch a flock!

ROBIN

Why are you waiting
for the wind?

CLERGYMAN

[*Taking up two little flags*]
Do you see

these two flags? One's the Union Jack,
the other is the Rattlesnake.
The wind will tell me which to fly.

ROBIN

I'm thinking of the absent one.
My kinsman, Major Molineux
is absent. The storms have hurt his house
lately. No one will help me find him.

CLERGYMAN

Perhaps the wind will blow him back.

ROBIN

I met a strange man, Colonel Greenough;
Half of his face was red, and half
was pocked. He said, "Wait here, and you
will meet your kinsman on his walk."

CLERGYMAN

You'd better wait here then. That red
and pocked man tends to speak the truth.

ROBIN

Why was his face two-colors, Father?

CLERGYMAN

He is an image of the city.
If his whole face turns red as blood,
We'll have to fly the Rattlesnake.

ROBIN

Say more about my kinsman, Father.
You said he was your friend and patron.

CLERGYMAN

Poor Molineux! he served the clergy
somewhat better than this city.
He had a special pew, you know.
He used to set a grand example.

ROBIN

He used to! You speak as if he were dead!

CLERGYMAN

Men blamed me, but I liked to watch
his red coat blazing like the sunset
at Sunday morning service here.
He was an easy-going fellow,
a lover of life, no Puritan.
He had invention, used to send
two six foot Privates here to help
with the collection. Yes, I had
to like him. He had his flaws, of course.

ROBIN

A red coat blazing like the sunrise,
that's how the Major was in Deerfield;
the gold lion of England shone
on his gilded carriage. He had a little
white scar like a question mark
on his right cheek. He got it killing
Frenchmen. He seemed to hold the world
like a gold ball in the palm of his hand.
Ours for the asking! All! We are
his last relations in the world!

CLERGYMAN

No one will dispute your claim.

ROBIN

The Major said he was the King's
intelligence in Massachusetts.

CLERGYMAN

No one will dispute his claim.
What shall we do with people? They
get worse and worse, but God improves.
God was green in Moses' time;
little by little though, he blossomed.
First came the prophets, then our Lord,
and then the Church.

ROBIN

The Church?

CLERGYMAN

The Church
gets more enlightened every day.
We've learned to disregard the Law
and look at persons. Who is my neighbor?
Anyone human is my neighbor. Sometimes
my neighbor is a man from Sodom.

[*Great noise of shouting.* ALL FORMER CHARACTERS, *except the*
MAN WITH THE MASK, *parade across the stage.* MOST OF THEM
wave Rattlesnake flags]

ROBIN

Father, I see two clergymen,
they're waving flags.

CLERGYMAN

I see my sign.

[*Snaps the whirligig with his thumb*]

Look, the wind has risen! Wherever
the spirit calls me, I must follow.

CROWD

Hurrah for the Republic!
Down with Major Molineux!

[*The* PEOPLE *sing a verse of Yankee Doodle, and draw* COLONEL
GREENOUGH *on stage in a red, white and blue cart. He stands
up and draws his sword. One can see that his face is now entirely red*]

MAN WITH MASK

The die is cast! I say, the die is cast.

ROBIN

Look at the Colonel,
his whole face is red as blood!

MAN WITH MASK

Major Molineux is coming.

CLERGYMAN

Are you sure we're strong enough?

MAN WITH MASK

Every British soldier in Boston
is killed or captured.

CROWD

Don't tread on me!
Don't tread on me! Don't tread on me!

My Kinsman, Major Molineux

ROBIN

What can I do to help my kinsman?

CLERGYMAN

Swap your flag and save your soul.

ROBIN

I want to save my kinsman, Father.

CLERGYMAN

No, no, Son, do as I do. Here, hold
this flag a moment, while I speak.

[*The* CLERGYMAN *hands* ROBIN *his Rattlesnake flag, tosses away
the whirligig, breaks his clay pipe, then takes a chair and
stands on it while he addresses the* CROWD *with both hands
raised. Throughout the crowd scene,* ROBIN *stands unconsciously holding the flag and suffering*]

How long, how long now, Men of Boston!
You've faced the furious tyrant's trident,
you've borne the blandishments of Sodom.
The Day of Judgment is at hand,
now we'll strip the scarlet whore,
King George shall swim in scarlet blood,
Now Nebuchadnezzar shall eat grass and die.
How long! How long! O Men of Boston,
behave like men, if you are men!

[*The* PEOPLE *cheer and take the* CLERGYMAN *on their shoulders*]

You've drawn the sword, Boys, throw away
the scabbard!

[*The* CLERGYMAN *draws a sword and throws down the scab-bard. Many of the* PEOPLE, *including the* PROSTITUTE, *draw swords and throw the scabbards rattling across the stage. They draw* MAJOR MOLINEUX *on stage in a red cart. He is partly tarred and feathered; one cheek is bleeding; his red British uniform is torn; he shakes with terror*]

ROBIN

Oh my kinsman, my dear kinsman,
they have wounded you!

MAN WITH MASK

Throw the boy from Deerfield out,
he has no garment for our wedding.

CLERGYMAN

No, let him stay, he is just a boy.

[ROBIN, *unthinking, holds the flag in front of him, while his eyes are fixed in horror and pity on the figure of the Major. The* BOY, *unconsciously, too, mingles among the* CROWD *without thinking. Someone asks him to give some dirt to throw at the* MAJOR *and he unthinkingly picks up some from a basket, and hands it to the* TAVERN KEEPER, *who throws it at the* MAJOR]

ROBIN

[*With a loud cry, but unconsciously waving the flag in his grief*]

Oh my poor kinsman, you are hurt!

CROWD

Don't tread on me! Don't tread on me!

My Kinsman, Major Molineux

[The MAJOR *slowly staggers to his feet. Slowly he stretches out his right arm and points to* ROBIN]

MAJOR MOLINEUX

Et tu, Brute!

TAVERN KEEPER

The Major wants to teach us Latin.

[The CROWD *laughs, and* ROBIN, *once more without thinking, laughs too, very loudly]*
*[*TAVERN KEEPER *goes up to the* MAJOR *and hands him a Rattlesnake flag]*

You're out of step, Sir. Here's your flag.

[The MAJOR *lurches a few steps from the cart, grinds the Rattlesnake underfoot, then turns and addresses the crowd]*

MAJOR MOLINEUX

Long live King George! Long live King George!
I'll sing until you cut my tongue out!

CROWD

Throw the Major in the river,
in the river, in the river!

[With a grating sound, the FERRYMAN *appears at the side of the stage, pushing the prow of his dory. The* MAJOR *staggers towards the* FERRYMAN]

MAJOR MOLINEUX

[To FERRYMAN]

Help me in my trouble. Let
me cross the river to my King!

[The FERRYMAN *stiffens.* THE MAN WITH THE MASK *throws him a silver crown]*

109

MAN WITH MASK

Ferryman, here's a silver crown,
take him or leave him, we don't care.

FERRYMAN

[*Still more threatening*]

The crown's no longer currency.

[*The* FERRYMAN *kicks the crown into the water*]

MAJOR MOLINEUX

Boatman, you rowed me here in state;
save me, now that I'm fallen!

FERRYMAN

There's no returning on my boat.

MAJOR MOLINEUX

[*Stretching out his hands and grappling the* FERRYMAN]

Save me in the name of God!

[*The* FERRYMAN *pushes the* MAJOR *off and hits him on the
head with his oar. The* MAJOR *screams, and lies still*]

FERRYMAN

He's crossed the river into his kingdom;
all tyrants must die as this man died.

[*One by one, the* PRINCIPAL CHARACTERS *come up and look at
the* MAJOR]

CLERGYMAN

He's dead. He had no time to pray.
I wish he'd called me. O Lord, remember

his past kindness to the Church;
all tyrants must die as this man died.

MAN IN PERIWIG

[*Taking the* MAJOR'S *empty scabbard*]

I have the Major's sword of office;
hem, hem, I have authority.

FIRST BARBER

His Honor has the hollow scabbard.

MAN IN PERIWIG

They build men right in England. Take him
all in all, he was a man;
all tyrants must die as this man died.

TAVERN KEEPER

[*Holding a poster*]

Look, this poster says the town
of Boston offers a thousand guineas
to anyone who kills the Major.
I'll take his wallet for the cause.
All tyrants must die as this man died.

PROSTITUTE

[*Taking the* MAJOR'S *hat*]

I'll need this hat to hide my head.
They build men right in England. Take him
all in all, he was a man;
all tyrants must die as this man died.

MAN WITH MASK

[*Plunging his sword in the* MAJOR]

Sic semper tyrannis!

FERRYMAN

His fare is paid now;
the Major's free to cross the river.

[*The* FERRYMAN *loads* MAJOR MOLINEUX'S *body on his boat,
and pushes off*]

CLERGYMAN

[*Coming up to* MAN WITH MASK]

Your hand! I want
to shake your hand, Sir. A great day!

MAN WITH MASK

Great and terrible! There's nothing
I can do about it now.

[*Turns to* ROBIN]

Here, boy, here's the Major's sword;
perhaps, you'll want a souvenir.

[CROWD *starts to leave.* ROBIN *and* BOY *alone*]

BOY

The Major's gone. We'll have to go
Back home. There's no one here to help us.

ROBIN

Yes, Major Molineux is dead.

[*Starts sadly towards the river*]

CROWD

Long live the Republic! Long live the Republic!

BOY

Look, Robin, I have found a flintlock.

[ROBIN *looks wistfully at the* CROWD, *now almost entirely gone.*
He pauses and then answers in a daze]

ROBIN

A flintlock?

BOY

Well, that's all I came to Boston for, I guess.
Let's go, I see the ferryman.

ROBIN

[*Still inattentive*]

I'm going.

[ROBIN *takes his brother's hand and turns firmly towards the*
city]

BOY

We are returning to the city!

[ALL THE PEOPLE *are gone now, the lights start to go out. A*
red sun shows on the river]

ROBIN

Yes, brother, we are staying here.
Look, the lights are going out,
the red sun's moving on the river.
Where will it take us to? . . . It's strange
to be here on our own—and free.

BOY

[*Sighting along his flintlock*]
Major Molineux is dead.

ROBIN
Yes, Major Molineux is dead.

CURTAIN

BENITO CERENO

ORIGINAL CAST FOR

Benito Cereno
Premiere November 1, 1964

Captain Amasa Delano: LESTER RAWLINS
John Perkins: JACK RYLAND
Don Benito Cereno: FRANK LANGELLA
Babu: ROSCOE LEE BROWNE
Atufal: CLAYTON CORBIN
Francesco: MICHAEL SCHULTZ
American Sailors: CONWAY W. YOUNG, ROBERT TINSLEY,
    RICHARD KJELLAND, E. EMMET WALSCH,
    HOWARD MARTIN
Spanish Sailors: LUKE ANDREAS, WILLIAM JACOBSON,
    JAMES ZAFERES
Negro Slaves: WOODIE KING, LONNIE STEVENS,
    GEORGE A. SHARPE, HURMAN FITZGERALD,
    ERNEST BAXTER, ASTON YOUNG, JUNE BROWN,
    MARY FOREMAN, GENE FOREMAN, JUDITH BYRD,
    M. S. MITCHELL, LANE FLOYD, PAUL PLUMMER,
    WALTER JONES, ETHAN COURTNEY

The scene

About the year 1800, an American sealing vessel, the *President Adams,* at anchor in an island harbor off the coast of Trinidad. The stage is part of the ship's deck. Everything is unnaturally clean, bare and ship-shape. To one side, a polished, coal-black cannon. The American captain, AMASA DELANO from Duxbury, Massachusetts, sits in a cane chair. He is a strong, comfortable looking man in his early thirties who wears a spotless blue coat and white trousers. Incongruously, he has on a straw hat and smokes a corncob pipe. Beside him stands JOHN PERKINS, his bosun, a very stiff, green young man, a relative of DELANO's. THREE SAILORS, one carrying an American flag, enter. EVERYONE stands at attention and salutes with machinelike exactitude. Then the THREE SAILORS march off-stage. DELANO and PERKINS are alone.

DELANO

There goes the most beautiful woman in South America.

PERKINS

We never see any women, Sir;
just this smothering, overcast Equator,
a seal or two,
the flat dull sea,
and a sky like a gray wasp's nest.

DELANO

I wasn't talking about women,
I was calling your attention to the American flag.

PERKINS

Yes, Sir! I wish we were home in Duxbury.

DELANO

We are home. America is wherever her flag flies.
My own deck is the only place in the world
where I feel at home.

PERKINS

That's too much for me, Captain Delano.
I mean I wish I were at home with my wife;
these world cruises are only for bachelors.

DELANO

Your wife will keep. You should smoke, Perkins.
Smoking turns men into philosophers
and swabs away their worries.
I can see my wife and children or not see them
in each puff of blue smoke.

PERKINS

You are always tempting me, Sir!
I try to keep fit,
I want to return to my wife as fit as I left her.

DELANO

You're much too nervous, Perkins.
Travel will shake you up. You should let
a little foreign dirt rub off on you.

I've taught myself to speak Spanish like a Spaniard.
At each South American port, they mistake me for a
Castilian Don.

PERKINS

Aren't you lowering yourself a little, Captain?
Excuse me, Sir, I have been wanting to ask you a question.
Don't you think our President, Mr. Jefferson, is
    lowering himself
by being so close to the French?
I'd feel a lot safer in this unprotected place
if we'd elected Mr. Adams instead of Mr. Jefferson.

DELANO

The better man ran second!
Come to think of it, he rather let us down
by losing the election just after we had named this ship,
the *President Adams*. Adams is a nervous dry fellow.
When you've travelled as much as I have,
you'll learn that that sort doesn't export, Perkins.
Adams didn't get a vote outside New England!

PERKINS

He carried every New England state;
that was better than winning the election.
I'm afraid I'm a dry fellow, too, Sir.

DELANO

Not when I've educated you!
When I am through with you, Perkins,
you'll be as worldly as the Prince Regent of England,
only you'll be a first class American officer.

121

I'm all for Jefferson, he has the popular touch.
Of course he's read too many books,
but I've always said an idea or two won't sink
    our Republic.
I'll tell you this, Perkins,
Mr. Jefferson is a gentleman and an American.

PERKINS

They say he has two illegitimate Negro children.

DELANO

The more the better! That's the quickest way
to raise the blacks to our level.
I'm surprised you swallow such Federalist bilge, Perkins!
I told you Mr. Jefferson is a gentleman and an American;
when a man's in office, Sir, we all pull behind him!

PERKINS

Thank God our Revolution ended where the French
    one began.

DELANO

Oh the French! They're like the rest of the Latins,
they're hardly white people,
they start with a paper republic
and end with a toy soldier, like Bonaparte.

PERKINS

Yes, Sir. I see a strange sail making for the harbor.
They don't know how to sail her.

DELANO

Hand me my telescope.

PERKINS

Aye, aye, Sir!

DELANO

[*With telescope*]

I see an ocean undulating in long scoops of swells;
it's set like the beheaded French Queen's high wig;
the sleek surface is like waved lead,
cooled and pressed in the smelter's mould.
I see flights of hurried gray fowl,
patches of fluffy fog.
They skim low and fitfully above the decks,
like swallows sabering flies before a storm.
This gray boat foreshadows something wrong.

PERKINS

It does, Sir!
They don't know how to sail her!

DELANO

I see a sulphurous haze above her cabin,
the new sun hangs like a silver dollar to her stern;
low creeping clouds blow on from them to us.

PERKINS

What else, Sir?

DELANO

The yards are woolly
the ship is furred with fog.
On the cracked and rotten head-boards,
the tarnished, gilded letters say, the *San Domingo*.

A rat's-nest messing up the deck,
black faces in white sheets are fussing with the ropes.
I think it's a cargo of Dominican monks.

PERKINS

Dominican monks, Sir! God help us,
I thought they were outlawed in the new world.

DELANO

No, it's nothing. I see they're only slaves.
The boat's transporting slaves.

PERKINS

Do you believe in slavery, Captain Delano?

DELANO

In a civilized country, Perkins,
everyone disbelieves in slavery,
everyone disbelieves in slavery and wants slaves.
We have the perfect uneasy answer;
in the North, we don't have them and want them;
Mr. Jefferson has them and fears them.

PERKINS

Is that how you answer, Sir,
when a little foreign dirt has rubbed off on you?

DELANO

Don't ask me such intense questions.
You should take up smoking, Perkins.
There was a beautiful, dumb English actress—
I saw her myself once in London.
They wanted her to look profound,

so she read Plato and the Bible and Benjamin Franklin,
and thought about them every minute.
She still looked like a moron.
Then they told her to think about nothing.
She thought about nothing, and looked like Socrates.
That's smoking, Perkins, you think about nothing and
    look deep.

PERKINS

I don't believe in slavery, Sir.

DELANO

You don't believe in slavery or Spaniards
or smoking or long cruises or monks or Mr. Jefferson!
You are a Puritan, all faith and fire.

PERKINS

Yes, Sir.

DELANO

God save America from Americans!

[*Takes up the telescope*]

I see octogonal network bagging out
from her heavy top like decayed beehives.
The battered forecastle looks like a raped Versailles.
On the stern-piece, I see the fading arms of Spain.
There's a masked satyr, or something
with its foot on a big white goddess.
She has quite a figure.

PERKINS

They oughtn't to be allowed on the ocean!

DELANO

Who oughtn't? Goddesses?

PERKINS

I mean Spaniards, who cannot handle a ship,
and mess up its hull with immoral statues.

DELANO

You're out of step. You're much too dry.
Bring me my three-cornered hat.
Order some men to clear a whaleboat.
I am going to bring water and fresh fish to the
    San Domingo.
These people have had some misfortune, Perkins!

PERKINS

Aye, aye, Sir.

DELANO

Spaniards? The name gets you down,
you think their sultry faces and language
make them Zulus.
You take the name Delano—
I've always thought it had some saving
Italian or Spanish virtue in it.

PERKINS

Yes, Sir.

DELANO

A Spaniard isn't a negro under the skin,
particularly a Spaniard from Spain—
these South American ones mix too much with the Indians.

Once you get inside a Spaniard,
he talks about as well as your wife in Duxbury.

PERKINS

[*Shouting*]

A boat for the captain! A whaleboat for Captain Delano!

[*A bosun's whistle is heard, the lights dim. When they come
up, we are on the deck of the* San Domingo, *the same set,
identical except for litter and disorder.* THREE AMERICAN SAIL-
ORS *climb on board. They are followed by* PERKINS *and* DELANO,
now wearing a three-cornered hat. Once on board, the AMER-
ICAN SAILORS *salute* DELANO *and stand stiffly at attention like
toys.* NEGROES *from the* San Domingo *drift silently and fur-
tively forward*]

DELANO

I see a wen of barnacles hanging to the waterline of
   this ship.
It sticks out like the belly of a pregnant woman.
Have a look at our dory Bosun.

PERKINS

Aye, aye, Sir!

[*By now, about twenty blacks and two Spanish sailors have
drifted in. They look like some gaudy, shabby, unnautical
charade, and pay no attention to the Americans, until an un-
seen figure in the rigging calls out a single sharp warning in
an unknown tongue. Then they all rush forward, shouting,
waving their arms and making inarticulate cries like birds.
Three shrill warnings come from the rigging. Dead silence.
The men from the* SAN DOMINGO *press back in a dense semi-
circle. One by one, individuals come forward, make showy
bows to* DELANO, *and speak*]

FIRST NEGRO

Scurvy, Master Yankee!

SECOND NEGRO

Yellow fever, Master Yankee!

THIRD NEGRO

Two men knocked overboard rounding Cape Horn,
Master Yankee!

FOURTH NEGRO

Nothing to eat, Master Yankee!

NEGRO WOMAN

Nothing to drink, Master Yankee!

SECOND NEGRO WOMAN

Our mouths are dead wood, Master Yankee!

DELANO

You see, Perkins,
these people have had some misfortune.

[*General hubbub, muttering, shouts, gestures, ritual and
dumbshow of distress. The rigging, hitherto dark, lightens,
as the sun comes out of a cloud, and shows* THREE OLD NE-
GROES, *identical down to their shabby patches. They perch
on cat's-heads; their heads are grizzled like dying willow tops;
each is picking bits of unstranded rope for oakum. It is they
who have been giving the warnings that control the people
below. Everyone,* DELANO *along with the rest, looks up.* DELANO
turns aside and speaks to PERKINS]

It is like a Turkish bazaar.

PERKINS

They are like gypsies showing themselves for money
at a county fair, Sir.

DELANO

This is enchanting after the blank gray roll of the ocean!
Go tell the Spanish captain I am waiting for him.

[PERKINS *goes off. Sharp warnings from the* OAKUM-PICKERS.
*A big black spread of canvas is pulled creakingly and cere-
moniously aside.* SIX FIGURES *stand huddled on a platform
about four feet from the deck. They look like weak old invalids in bathrobes and nightcaps until they strip to the waist
and turn out to be huge, shining young negroes. Saying nothing, they set to work cleaning piles of rusted hatchets. From
time to time, they turn and clash their hatchets together with
a rhythmic shout.* PERKINS *returns*]

PERKINS

Their captain's name is Don Benito Cereno,
he sends you his compliments, Sir.
He looks more like a Mexican planter than a seaman.
He's put his fortune on his back:
he doesn't look as if he had washed since they left port.

DELANO

Did you tell him I was waiting for him?
A captain should be welcomed by his fellow-captain.
I can't understand this discourtesy.

PERKINS

He's coming, but there's something wrong with him.

[BENITO CERENO, *led by his negro servant,* BABU, *enters.* BENITO,

looking sick and dazed, is wearing a sombrero and is dressed
with a singular but shabby richness. Head bent to one side,
he leans in a stately coma against the rail, and stares unsee-
ingly at DELANO. BABU, *all in scarlet, and small and quick,*
keeps whispering, pointing and pulling at BENITO'S *sleeve.*
DELANO *walks over to them]*

DELANO

Your hand, Sir. I am Amasa Delano,
captain of the *President Adams,*
a sealing ship from the United States.
This is your lucky day,
the sun is out of hiding for the first time in two weeks,
and here I am aboard your ship
like the Good Samaritan with fresh food and water.

BENITO

The Good Samaritan? Yes, yes,
we mustn't use the Scriptures lightly.
Welcome, Captain. It is the end of the day.

DELANO

The end? It's only morning.
I loaded and lowered a whaleboat
as soon as I saw how awkwardly your ship was making for
    the harbor.

BENITO

Your whaleboat's welcome, Captain.
I am afraid I am still stunned by the storm.

DELANO

Buck up. Each day is a new beginning.
Assign some sailors to help me dole out my provisions.

BENITO

I have no sailors.

BABU

[*In a quick sing-song:*]

Scurvy, yellow fever,
ten men knocked off on the Horn,
doldrums, nothing to eat, nothing to drink!
By feeding us, you are feeding the King of Spain.

DELANO

Sir, your slave has a pretty way of talking.
What do you need?

[DELANO *waits for* BENITO *to speak. When nothing more is
said, he shifts awkwardly from foot to foot, then turns to his*
SAILORS]

Stand to, men!

[*The* AMERICAN SAILORS, *who have been lounging and gaping,
stand in a row, as if a button had been pressed*]

Lay our fish and water by the cabin!

[*The* SAILORS *arrange the watercans and baskets of fish by
the cabin. A sharp whistle comes from the* OAKUM-PICKERS.
Almost instantly, the provisions disappear]

Captain Cereno, you are surely going to taste my water!

BENITO

A captain is a servant, almost a slave, Sir.

DELANO

No, a captain's a captain.

I am sending for more provisions.
Stand to!

[*The* AMERICAN SAILORS *stand to*]

Row back to the ship. When you get there,
take on five hogsheads of fresh water,
and fifty pounds of soft bread.

[FIRST SAILOR *salutes and goes down the ladder*]

Bring all our remaining pumpkins!

[SECOND *and* THIRD SAILORS *salute and go down the ladder*]

My bosun and I will stay on board,
until our boat returns.
I imagine you can use us.

BENITO

Are you going to stay here alone?
Won't your ship be lost without you?
Won't you be lost without your ship?

BABU

Listen to Master!
He is the incarnation of courtesy, Yankee Captain.
Your ship doesn't need you as much as we do.

DELANO

Oh, I've trained my crew.
I can sail my ship in my sleep.

[*Leaning over the railing and calling*]

Men, bring me a box of lump sugar,
and six bottles of my best cider.

[*Turning to* BENITO]

Cider isn't my favorite drink, Don Benito,
but it's a New England specialty;
I'm ordering six bottles for your table.

[BABU *whispers and gestures to* DON BENITO, *who is exhausted
and silent*]

BABU

Une bouteille du vin [*to* NEGROES]
My master wishes to give you a bottle
of the oldest wine in Seville.

[*He whistles. A negro woman rushes into the cabin and returns with a dusty beribboned bottle, which she holds like
a baby*]
[BABU *ties a rope around the bottle*]

BABU

I am sending this bottle of wine to your cabin.
When you drink it, you will remember us.
Do you see these ribbons? The crown of Spain is tied
    to one.
Forgive me for tying a rope around the King of
    Spain's neck.

[*Lowers the wine on the rope to the whaleboat*]

DELANO

[*Shouting to his* SAILORS]

Pick up your oars!

SAILORS

Aye, aye, Sir!

We're New England Federalists;
we can drink the King of Spain's health.

[BENITO *stumbles off-stage on* BABU'S *arm*]

PERKINS

Captain Cereno hasn't travelled as much as you have;
I don't think he knew what you meant by the New England
Federalists.

DELANO

[*Leaning comfortably on the rail; half to himself and half to*
PERKINS]

The wind is dead. We drift away.
We will be left alone all day,
here in this absentee empire.
Thank God, I know my Spanish!

PERKINS

You'll have to watch them, Sir.
Brown men in charge of black men—
it doesn't add up to much!
This Babu, I don't trust him!
Why doesn't he talk with a Southern accent,
Like Mr. Jefferson? They're out of hand, Sir!

DELANO

Nothing relaxes order more than misery.
They need severe superior officers.
They haven't one.

Now, if this Benito were a man of energy . . .
a Yankee . . .

PERKINS

How can a Spaniard sail?

DELANO

Some can. There was Vasco da Gama and Columbus . . .
No, I guess they were Italians. Some can,
but this captain is tubercular.

PERKINS

Spaniards and Negroes have no business on a ship.

DELANO

Why is this captain so indifferent to me?
If only I could stomach his foreign reserve!
This absolute dictator of his ship
only gives orders through his slaves!
He is like some Jesuit-haunted Hapsburg king
about to leave the world and hope the world will end.

PERKINS

He said he was lost in the storm.

DELANO

Perhaps it's only policy,
a captain's icy dignity
obliterating all democracy—

PERKINS

He's like someone walking in his sleep.

DELANO

Ah, slumbering dominion!
He is so self-conscious in his imbecility . . .
No, he's sick. He sees his men no more than me.
This ship is like a crowded immigration boat;
it needs severe superior officers,
the friendly arm of a strong mate.
Perhaps, I ought to take it over by force.
No, they're sick, they've been through the plague.
I'll go and speak and comfort my fellow captain.
I think you can help me, Captain. I'm feeling useless.
My own thoughts oppress me, there's so much to do.
I wonder if you would tell me the whole sad story of
     your voyage.
Talk to me as captain to captain.
We have sailed the same waters.
Please tell me your story.

BENITO

A story? A story! That's out of place.
When I was a child, I used to beg for stories back in Lima.
Now my tongue's tied and my heart is bleeding.

> [*Stops talking, as if his breath were gone. He stares for a few
> moments, then looks up at the rigging, as if he were counting
> the ropes one by one.* DELANO *turns abruptly to* PERKINS]

DELANO

Go through the ship, Perkins,
and see if you can find me a Spaniard who can talk.

BENITO

You must be patient, Captain Delano;

136

if we only see with our eyes,
sometimes we cannot see at all.

DELANO

I stand corrected, Captain;
tell me about your voyage.

BENITO

It's now a hundred and ninety days . . .
This ship, well manned, well officered, with several
      cabin passengers,
carrying a cargo of Paraguay tea and Spanish cutlery.
That parcel of Negro slaves, less than four score now,
was once three hundred souls.
Ten sailors and three officers fell from the mainyard off
      the Horn;
part of our rigging fell overboard with them,
as they were beating down the icy sail.
We threw away all our cargo,
Broke our waterpipes,
Lashed them on deck
this was the chief cause of our suffering.

DELANO

I must interrupt you, Captain.
How did you happen to have three officers on
      the mainyard?
I never heard of such a disposal,
it goes against all seamanship.

BABU

Our officers never spared themselves;

if there was any danger, they rushed in
to save us without thinking.

DELANO

I can't understand such an oversight.

BABU

There was no oversight. My master had a hundred eyes.
He had an eye for everything.
Sometimes the world falls on a man.
The sea wouldn't let Master act like a master,
yet he saved himself and many lives.
He is still a rich man, and he saved the ship.

BENITO

Oh my God, I wish the world had fallen on me,
and the terrible cold sea had drowned me;
that would have been better than living through what I've
lived through!

BABU

He is a good man, but his mind is off;
he's thinking about the fever when the wind stopped—
poor, poor Master!
Be patient, Yankee Captain, these fits are short,
Master will be the master once again.

BENITO

The scurvy was raging through us.
We were on the Pacific. We were invalids
and couldn't man our mangled spars.
A hurricane blew us northeast through the fog.
Then the wind died.

We lay in irons fourteen days in unknown waters,
our black tongues stuck through our mouths,
but we couldn't mend our broken waterpipes.

BABU

Always those waterpipes,
he dreams about them like a pile of snakes!

BENITO

Yellow fever followed the scurvy,
the long heat thickened in the calm,
my Spaniards turned black and died like slaves,
The blacks died too. I am my only officer left.

BABU

Poor, poor Master! He had a hundred eyes,
he lived our lives for us.
He is still a rich man.

BENITO

In the smart winds beating us northward,
our torn sails dropped like sinkers in the sea;
each day we dropped more bodies.
Almost without a crew, canvas, water, or a wind,
we were bounced about by the opposing waves
through cross-currents and the weedy calms,
and dropped our dead.
Often we doubled and redoubled on our track
like children lost in jungle. The thick fog
hid the Continent and our only port from us.

BABU

We were poor kidnapped jungle creatures.

We only lived on what he could give us.
He had a hundred eyes, he was the master.

BENITO

These Negroes saved me, Captain.
Through the long calamity,
they were as gentle as their owner, Don Aranda, promised.
Don Aranda took away their chains before he died.

BABU

Don Aranda saved our lives, but we couldn't save his.
Even in Africa I was a slave.
He took away my chains.

BENITO

I gave them the freedom of my ship.
I did not think they were crates or cargo or cannibals.
But it was Babu—under God, I swear I owe my life
        to Babu!
He calmed his ignorant, wild brothers,
never left me, saved the *San Domingo*.

BABU

Poor, poor Master. He is still a rich man.
Don't speak of Babu. Babu is the dirt under your feet.
He did his best.

DELANO

You are a good fellow, Babu.
You are the salt of the earth. I envy you, Don Benito;
he is no slave, Sir, but your friend.

BENITO

Yes, he is salt in my wounds.
I can never repay him, I mean.
Excuse me, Captain, my strength is gone.
I have done too much talking. I want to rest.

[BABU *leads* BENITO *to a shabby straw chair at the side.* BENITO *sits.* BABU *fans him with his sombrero*]

PERKINS

He's a fine gentleman, but no seaman.
A cabin boy would have known better
than to send his three officers on the mainyard.

DELANO

[*Paying no attention*]

A terrible story. I would have been unhinged myself.

[*Looking over toward* BABU *and* BENITO]

There's a true servant. They do things better
in the South and in South America—
trust in return for trust!
The beauty of that relationship is unknown
in New England. We're too much alone
in Massachusetts, Perkins.
How do our captains and our merchants live,
each a republic to himself.
Even Sam Adams had no friends and only loved the mob.

PERKINS

Sir, you are forgetting that
New England seamanship brought them their slaves.

DELANO

Oh, just our Southern slaves;
we had nothing to do with these fellows.

PERKINS

The ocean would be a different place
if every Spaniard served an apprenticeship on an
     American ship
before he got his captain's papers.

DELANO

This captain's a gentleman, not a sailor.
His little yellow hands
got their command before they held a rope—
in by the cabin-window, not the hawse-hole!
Do you want to know why
they drifted hog-tied in those easy calms—
inexperience, sickness, impotence and aristocracy!

PERKINS

Here comes Robinson Crusoe and his good man Friday.

DELANO

We don't beat a man when he's down.

[BENITO *advances uncertainly on* BABU's *arm*]

I am glad to see you on your feet again,
That's the only place for a Captain, sir!
I have the cure for you, I have decided
to bring you medicine and a sufficient supply of water.
A first class deck officer, a man from Salem,
shall be stationed on your quarter deck,

142

a temporary present from my owners.
We shall refit your ship and clear this mess.

BENITO

You will have to clear away the dead.

BABU

This excitement is bad for him, Yankee Master.
He's lived with death. He lives on death still;
this sudden joy will kill him. You've heard
how thirsty men die from overdrinking!
His heart is with his friend, our owner, Don Aranda.

BENITO

I am the only owner.

> [*He looks confused and shaken*]
> [BABU *scurries off and brings up the straw chair.* BENITO *sits*]

DELANO

Your friend is dead? He died of fever?

BENITO

He died very slowly and in torture.
He was the finest man in Lima.
We were brought up together,
I am lost here.

DELANO

Pardon me, Sir. You are young at sea.
My experience tells me what your trouble is:
this is the first body you have buried in the ocean.
I had a friend like yours, a warm honest fellow,
who would look you in the eye—

we had to throw him to the sharks.
Since then I've brought embalming gear on board.
Each man of mine shall have a Christian grave on land.
You wouldn't shake so, if Don Aranda were on board,
I mean, if you'd preserved the body.

BENITO

If he were on board this ship?
If I had preserved his body?

BABU

Be patient, Master!
We still have the figurehead.

DELANO

You have the figurehead?

BABU

You see that thing wrapped up in black cloth?
It's a figurehead Don Aranda bought us in Spain.
It was hurt in the storm. It's very precious.
Master takes comfort in it,
he is going to give it to Don Aranda's widow.
It's time for the pardon ceremony, Master.

[*Sound of clashing hatchets*]

DELANO

I am all for these hatchet-cleaners.
They are saving cargo. They make
an awful lot of pomp and racket though
about a few old, rusty knives.

144

BENITO

They think steel is worth its weight in gold.

[*A slow solemn march is sounded on the gongs and other instruments. A gigantic coal-black* NEGRO *comes up the steps. He wears a spiked iron collar to which a chain is attached that goes twice around his arms and ends padlocked to a broad band of iron. The* NEGRO *comes clanking forward and stands dumbly and like a dignitary in front of* BENITO. *Two small black boys bring* BENITO *a frail rattan cane and a silver ball, which they support on a velvet cushion.* BENITO *springs up, holds the ball, and raises the cane rigidly above the head of the negro in chains. For a moment, he shows no trace of sickness. The assembled blacks sing, "Evviva, Benito!" three times*]

BABU

[*At one side with the Americans, but keeping an eye on* BENITO]

You are watching the humiliation of King Atufal,
once a ruler in Africa. He ruled as much land there
    as your President.
Poor Babu was a slave even in Africa,
a black man's slave, and now a white man's.

BENITO

[*In a loud, firm voice*]

Former King Atufal, I call on you to kneel!
Say, "My sins are black as night,
I ask the King of Spain's pardon
through his servant, Don Benito."

[*Pause.* ATUFAL *doesn't move*]

NEGROES

Your sins are black as night, King Atufal!
Your sins are black as night, King Atufal!

BENITO

What has King Atufal done?

BABU

I will tell you later, Yankee Captain.

BENITO

Ask pardon, former King Atufal.
If you will kneel,
I will strike away your chains.

[ATUFAL *slowly raises his chained arms and lets them drop*]

Ask pardon!

WOMAN SLAVE

Ask pardon King Atufal.

BENITO

Go!

[*Sound of instruments. The* BLACK BOYS *take* BENITO's *ball and cane. The straw chair is brought up.* BENITO *sits.* FRANCESCO *then leads him off-stage*]

BABU

Francesco!
I will be with you in a moment, Master.
You mustn't be afraid,
Francesco will serve you like a second Babu.

146

BENITO

Everyone serves me alike here,
but no one can serve me as you have.

BABU

I will be with you in a moment.
The Yankee master is at sea on our ship.
He wants me to explain our customs.

[BENITO *is carried off-stage*]

You would think Master's afraid of dying,
if Babu leaves him!

DELANO

I can imagine your tenderness during his sickness.
You were part of him,
you were almost a wife.

BABU

You say such beautiful things,
the United States must be a paradise for people like Babu.

DELANO

I don't know.
We have our faults. We have many states,
some of them could stand improvement.

BABU

The United States must be heaven.

DELANO

I suppose we have fewer faults than other countries.
What did King Atufal do?

BABU

He used the Spanish flag for toilet paper.

DELANO

That's treason.
Did Atufal know what he was doing?
Perhaps the flag was left somewhere it shouldn't have been.
Things aren't very strict here.

BABU

I never thought of that.
I will go and tell Master.

DELANO

Oh, no, you mustn't do that!
I never interfere with another man's ship.
Don Benito is your lord and dictator.
How long has this business with King Atufal been
    going on?

BABU

Ever since the yellow fever,
and twice a day.

DELANO

He did a terrible thing, but he looks like a royal fellow.
You shouldn't call him a king, though,
it puts ideas into his head.

BABU

Atufal had gold wedges in his ears in Africa;
now he wears a padlock and Master bears the key.

148

DELANO

I see you have a feeling for symbols of power.
You had better be going now,
Don Benito will be nervous about you.

[BABU *goes off*]

That was a terrible thing to do with a flag;
everything is untidy and unravelled here—
this sort of thing would never happen on the
    President Adams.

PERKINS

Your ship is as shipshape as our country, Sir.

DELANO

I wish people wouldn't take me as representative of
    our country:
America's one thing, I am another;
we shouldn't have to bear one another's burdens.

PERKINS

You are a true American for all your talk, Sir;
I can't believe you were mistaken for a Castilian Don.

DELANO

No one would take me for Don Benito.

PERKINS

I wonder if he isn't an imposter, some traveling actor from
    a circus?

DELANO

No, Cereno is a great name in Peru, like Winthrop or
    Adams with us.

149

I recognize the family features in our captain.

[*An* OLD SPANISH SAILOR, *grizzled and dirty, is seen crawling on all fours with an armful of knots toward the Americans. He points to where* BENITO *and* BABU *have disappeared and whistles. He holds up the knots as though he were in chains, then throws them out loosely on the deck in front of him. A* GROUP OF NEGROES *forms a circle around him, holding hands and singing childishly. Then, laughing, they carry the* SPANIARD *off-stage on their shoulders*]

These blacks are too familiar!
We are never alone!

[*Sound of gongs. Full minute's pause, as if time were passing.* DELANO *leans on the railing. The sun grows brighter*]

This ship is strange.
These people are too spontaneous—all noise and show,
no character!
Real life is a simple monotonous thing.
I wonder about that story about the calms;
it doesn't stick.
Don Benito hesitated himself in telling it.
No one could run a ship so stupidly,
and place three officers on one yard.

[BENITO *and* BABU *return*]

A captain has unpleasant duties;
I am sorry for you, Don Benito.

BENITO
You find my ship unenviable, Sir?

DELANO

I was talking about punishing Atufal;
he acted like an animal!

BENITO

Oh, yes, I was forgetting . . .
He was a King,
How long have you lain in at this island, Sir?

DELANO

Oh, a week today.

BENITO

What was your last port, Sir?

DELANO

Canton.

BENITO

You traded seal-skins and American muskets
for Chinese tea and silks, perhaps?

DELANO

We took in some silks.

BENITO

A little gold and silver too?

DELANO

Just a little silver. We are only merchants.
We take in a dollar here and there. We have no Peru,
or a Pizarro who can sweat gold out of the natives.

BENITO

You'll find things have changed

a little in Peru since Pizarro, Captain.

[*Starts to move away.* BABU *whispers to him, and he comes back abruptly, as if he had forgotten something important*]

How many men have you on board, Sir?

DELANO

Some twenty-five, Sir. Each man is at his post.

BENITO

They're all on board, Sir, now?

DELANO

They're all on board. Each man is working.

BENITO

They'll be on board tonight, Sir?

DELANO

Tonight? Why do you ask, Don Benito?

BENITO

Will they all be on board tonight, Captain?

DELANO

They'll be on board for all I know.

[PERKINS *makes a sign to* DELANO]

Well, no, to tell the truth, today's our Independence Day.
A gang is going ashore to see the village.
A little diversion improves their efficiency,
a little regulated corruption.

BENITO

You North Americans take no chances. Generally,
    I suppose,
even your merchant ships go more or less armed?

DELANO

A rack of muskets, sealing spears and cutlasses.
Oh, and a six-pounder or two; we are a sealing ship,
but with us each merchant is a privateer—
only in case of oppression, of course.
You've heard about how we shoot pirates.

BABU

Boom, boom, come Master.

> [BENITO *walks away on* BABU'S *arm and sits down, almost off-
> stage in his straw chair. They whisper. Meanwhile, a* SPANISH
> SAILOR *climbs the rigging furtively, spread-eagles his arms and
> shows a lace shirt under his shabby jacket. He points to*
> BENITO *and* BABU *and winks. At a cry from* ONE OF THE OAKUM
> PICKERS, THREE NEGROES *help the* SPANIARD *down with servile,
> ceremonious attentions*]

PERKINS

Did you see that sailor's lace shirt, Sir?
He must have robbed one of the cabin passengers.
I hear that people strip the dead
in these religious countries.

DELANO

No, you don't understand the Spaniards.
In these old Latin countries,
each man's a beggar or a noble, often both;
they have no middle class. With them it's customary

153

to sew a mess of gold and pearls on rags—
that's how an aristocracy that's going to the dogs
keeps up its nerve.

DELANO

It's odd though,
that Spanish sailor seemed to want to tell me something.
He ought to dress himself properly and speak his mind.
That's what we do. That's why we're strong:
everybody trusts us. Nothing gets done
when every man's a noble. I wonder why
the captain asked me all those questions?

PERKINS

He was passing the time of day, Sir;
It's a Latin idleness.

DELANO

It's strange. Did you notice how Benito stopped rambling?
He was conventional . . . consecutive for the first time
        since we met him.
Something's wrong. Perhaps, they've men below the decks,
a sleeping volcano of Spanish infantry. The Malays do it,
play sick and cut your throat.
A drifting boat, a dozen doped beggars on deck,
two hundred sweating murderers packed below
        like sardines—
that's rot! Anyone can see these people are really sick,
sicker than usual. Our countries are at peace.
I wonder why he asked me all those questions?

PERKINS

Just idle curiosity. I hear
the gentlemen of Lima sit at coffee-tables from sun to sun
and gossip. They don't even have women to look at;
they're all locked up with their aunts.

DELANO

Their sun is going down. These old empires go.
They are much too familiar with their blacks.
I envy them though, they have no character,
they feel no need to stand alone.
We stand alone too much,
that's why no one can touch us for sailing a ship;
When a country loses heart, it's easier to live.
Ah, Babu! I suppose Don Benito's indisposed again!
Tell him I want to talk to his people;
there's nothing like a well man to help the sick.

BABU

Master is taking his siesta, Yankee Master.
His siesta is sacred, I am afraid to disturb it.
Instead, let me show you our little entertainment.

DELANO

Let's have your entertainment;
if you know a man's pleasure
you know his measure.

BABU

We are a childish people. Our pleasures are childish.
No one helped us, we know nothing

about your important amusements,
such as killing seals and pirates.

DELANO

I'm game. Let's have your entertainment.

> [BABU *signals. The gong sounds ten times and the canvas is
> pulled from the circular structure. Enclosed in a triangular
> compartment, an* OLD SPANISH SAILOR *is dipping naked white
> dolls in a tar-pot*]

BABU

This little amusement keeps him alive, Yankee Master.
He is especially fond of cleaning the dolls
after he has dirtied them.

> [*The* OLD SPANISH SAILOR *laughs hysterically, and then smears
> his whole face with tar*]

OLD SPANISH SAILOR

My soul is white!

BABU

The yellow fever destroyed his mind.

DELANO

Let's move on. This man's brain,
as well as his face, is defiled with pitch!

BABU

He says his soul is white.

> [*The structure is pushed around and another triangular com-
> partment appears. A* NEGRO BOY *is playing chess against a
> splendid Spanish doll with a crown on its head. He stops and
> holds two empty wine bottles to his ears*]

This boy is deaf.
The yellow fever destroyed his mind.

DELANO

Why is he holding those bottles to his ears?

BABU

He is trying to be a rabbit,
or listening to the ocean, his mother—
who knows?

DELANO

If he's deaf, how can he hear the ocean?
Anyway, he can't hear me.
I pass, let's move on.

> [*The structure is pushed around to a third compartment. A* SPANISH SAILOR *is holding a big armful of rope*]

What are you knotting there, my man?

SPANISH SAILOR

The knot.

DELANO

So I see, but what's it for?

SPANISH SAILOR

For someone to untie. Catch!

> [*Throws the knot to* DELANO]

BABU

> [*Snatching the knot from* DELANO]

It's dirty, it will dirty your uniform.

157

DELANO

Let's move on. Your entertainment
is rather lacking in invention, Babu.

BABU

We have to do what we can
We are just beginners at acting.
This next one will be better.

[*The structure is pushed around and shows a beautiful* NEGRO
WOMAN. *She is dressed and posed as the Virgin Mary. A Christmas crèche is arranged around her. A* VERY WHITE SPANIARD
*dressed as Saint Joseph stands behind her. She holds a Christ-
child, the same crowned doll, only black, the* NEGRO BOY *was
playing chess against*]

She is the Virgin Mary. That man is not the father.

DELANO

I see. I suppose her son is the King of Spain.

BABU

The Spaniards taught us everything,
there's nothing we can learn from you, Yankee Master.
When they took away our country, they gave us a
    better world.
Things do not happen in that world as they do here.

DELANO

That's a very beautiful,
though unusual Virgin Mary.

BABU

Yes, the Bible says, "I am black not white."
When Don Aranda was dying,

158

we wanted to give him the Queen of Heaven
because he took away our chains.

PERKINS

The Spaniards must have taught them everything;
they're all mixed up, they don't even know their religion.

DELANO

No, no! The Catholic Church doesn't just teach,
it knows how to take from its converts.

BABU

Do you want to shake hands with the Queen of Heaven,
    Yankee Master?

DELANO

No, I'm not used to royalty.
Tell her I believe in freedom of religion,
if people don't take liberties.
Let's move on.

BABU

    [*Kneeling to the Virgin Mary*]

I present something Your Majesty has never seen,
a white man who doesn't believe in taking liberties,
Your Majesty.

    [*The structure is pushed around and shows* ATUFAL *in chains
    but with a crown on his head*]

BABU

This is the life we believe in.

Ask pardon, King Atufal!
Kiss the Spanish flag!

DELANO

Please don't ask me to shake hands with King Atufal!

[*The canvas is put back on the structure*]

BABU

You look tired and serious, Yankee Master.
We have to have what fun we can.
We never would have lived through the deadly calms
without a little amusement.

[*Bows and goes off*]
[*The* NEGROES *gradually drift away.* DELANO *sighs with relief*]

DELANO

Well, that wasn't much!
I suppose Shakespeare started that way.

PERKINS

Who cares?
I see a speck on the blue sea, Sir,
our whaleboat is coming.

DELANO

A speck? My eyes are speckled.
I seem to have been dreaming. What's solid?

[*Touches the ornate railing; a piece falls onto the deck*]

This ship is nothing, Perkins!
I dreamed someone was trying to kill me!
How could he? Jack-of-the-beach,

they used to call me on the Duxbury shore.
Carrying a duck-satchel in my hand, I used to paddle
along the waterfront from a hulk to school.
I didn't learn much there. I was always shooting duck
or gathering huckleberries along the marsh with
      Cousin Nat!
I like nothing better than breaking myself on the surf.
I used to track the seagulls down the five-mile stretch
      of beach for eggs.
How can I be killed now at the ends of the earth
by this insane Spaniard?
Who could want to murder Amasa Delano?
My conscience is clean. God is good.
What am I doing on board this nigger-pirate ship?

PERKINS

You're not talking like a skipper, Sir.
Our boat's a larger spot now.

DELANO

I am childish.
I am doddering and drooling into my second childhood.
God help me, nothing's solid!

PERKINS

Don Benito, Sir. Touch him,
he's as solid as his ship.

DELANO

Don Benito? He's a walking ghost!

[BENITO *comes up to* DELANO. BABU *is a few steps behind him*]

161

BENITO

I am the ghost of myself, Captain.
Excuse me, I heard you talking about dreams
    and childhood.
I was a child, too, once, I have dreams about it.

DELANO

[*Starting*]

I'm sorry.
This jumping's just a nervous habit.
I thought you were part of my dreams.

BENITO

I was taking my siesta,
I dreamed I was a boy back in Lima.
I was with my brothers and sisters,
and we were dressed for the festival of Corpus Christi
like people at our Bourbon court.
We were simple children, but something went wrong;
little black men came on us with beetle backs.
They had caterpillar heads and munched away on our
    fine clothes.
They made us lick their horned and varnished insect legs.
Our faces turned brown from their spit,
we looked like bugs, but nothing could save our lives!

DELANO

Ha, ha, Captain. We are like two dreams meeting head-on.
My whaleboat's coming,
we'll both feel better over a bottle of cider.

[BABU *blows a bosun's whistle. The gongs are sounded with descending notes. The* NEGROES *assemble in ranks*]

BABU

It's twelve noon, Master Yankee.
Master wants his midday shave.

ALL THE NEGROES

Master wants his shave! Master wants his shave!

BENITO

Ah, yes, the razor! I have been talking too much.
You can see how badly I need a razor.
I must leave you, Captain.

BABU

No, Don Amasa wants to talk.
Come to the cabin, Don Amasa.
Don Amasa will talk, Master will listen.
Babu will lather and strop.

DELANO

I want to talk to you about navigation.
I am new to these waters.

BENITO

Doubtless, doubtless, Captain Delano.

PERKINS

I think I'll take my siesta, Sir.

> [*He walks off*]
> [BENITO, BABU, *and* DELANO *walk toward the back of the stage.
> A scrim curtain lifts, showing a light deck cabin that forms
> a sort of attic. The floor is matted, partitions that still leave*

splintered traces have been knocked out. To one side, a small
table screwed to the floor; on it, a dirty missal; above it, a
small crucifix, rusty crossed muskets on one side, rusty crossed
cutlasses on the other. BENITO *sits down in a broken throne-*
like and gilded chair. BABU *begins to lather. A magnificent*
array of razors, bottles and other shaving equipment lies on
a table beside him. Behind him, a hammock with a pole in it
and a dirty pillow]

DELANO

So this is where you took your siesta.

BENITO

Yes, Captain, I rest here when my fate will let me.

DELANO

This seems like a sort of dormitory, sitting-room,
sail-loft, chapel, armory, and private bedroom all together.

BENITO

Yes, Captain: events have not been favorable
to much order in my personal arrangements.

[BABU *moves back and opens a locker. A lot of flags, torn shirts*
and socks tumble out. He takes one of the flags, shakes it with
a flourish, and ties it around BENITO's *neck*]

BABU

Master needs more protection.
I do everything I can to save his clothes.

DELANO

The Castle and the Lion of Spain.
Why, Don Benito, this is the flag of Spain you're using!
It's well it's only I and not the King of Spain who sees this!

164

All's one, though, I guess, in this carnival world.
I see you like gay colors as much as Babu.

BABU

[*Giggling*]

The bright colors draw the yellow fever
from Master's mind.

[*Raises the razor*]
[BENITO *begins to shake*]

Now, Master, now, Master!

BENITO

You are talking while you hold the razor.

BABU

You mustn't shake so, Master.
Look, Don Amasa, Master always shakes when I shave him,
though he is braver than a lion and stronger than a castle.
Master knows Babu has never yet drawn blood.
I may, though, sometime, if he shakes so much.
Now, Master!
Come, Don Amasa, talk to Master about the gales
and calms,
he'll answer and forget to shake.

DELANO

Those calms, the more I think of them the more I wonder.
You say you were two months sailing here;
I made that stretch in less than a week.
We never met with any calms.

If I'd not heard your story from your lips,
and seen your ruined ship,
I would have said something was missing,
I would have said this was a mystery ship.

BENITO

For some men the whole world is a mystery;
they cannot believe their senses.

[BENITO *shakes, the razor gets out of hand and cuts his cheek*]

Santa Maria!

BABU

Poor, poor Master, see, you shook so;
this is Babu's first blood.
Please answer Don Amasa, while I wipe
this ugly blood from the razor and strop it again.

BENITO

The sea was like the final calm of the world
On, on it went. It sat on us and drank our strength,
crosscurrents eased us out to sea,
the yellow fever changed our blood to poison.

BABU

You stood by us. Some of us stood by you!

BENITO

Yes, my Spanish crew was weak and surly, but the blacks,
the blacks were angels. Babu has kept me in this world.
I wonder what he is keeping me for?
You belong to me. I belong to you forever.

166

BABU

Ah, Master, spare yourself.
Forever is a very long time;
nothing's forever.

[*With great expertness, delicacy and gentleness,* BABU *massages* BENITO's *cheeks, shakes out the flag, pours lotion from five bottles on* BENITO's *hair, cleans the shaving materials, and stands off admiring his work*]

Master looks just like a statue.
He's like a figurehead, Don Amasa!

[DELANO *looks, then starts to walk out leaving* BENITO *and* BABU. *The curtain drops upon them.* DELANO *rejoins* PERKINS, *lounging at the rail*]

PERKINS

Our boat is coming.

DELANO

[*Gaily*]

I know!
I don't know how I'll explain this pomp
and squalor to my own comfortable family of a crew.
Even shaving here is like a High Mass.
There's something in a Negro, something
that makes him fit to have around your person.
His comb and brush are castanets.
. What tact Babu had!
What noiseless, gliding briskness!

PERKINS

Our boat's about along side, Sir.

DELANO

What's more, the Negro has a sense of humor.
I don't mean their boorish giggling and teeth-showing,
I mean his easy cheerfulness in every glance and gesture.
You should have seen Babu toss that Spanish flag like
     a juggler,
and change it to a shaving napkin!

PERKINS

The boat's here, Sir.

DELANO

We need inferiors, Perkins,
more manners, more docility, no one has an inferior mind
     in America.

PERKINS

Here is your crew, Sir.

[BABU *runs out from the cabin. His cheek is bleeding*]

DELANO

Why, Babu, what has happened?

BABU

Master will never get better from his sickness.
His bad nerves and evil fever made him use me so.
I gave him one small scratch by accident,
the only time I've nicked him, Don Amasa.
He cut me with his razor. Do you think I will die?
I'd rather die than bleed to death!

DELANO

It's just a pinprick, Babu. You'll live.

168

BABU

I must attend my master.

[*Runs back into cabin*]

DELANO

Just a pinprick, but I wouldn't have thought
Don Benito had the stuff to swing a razor.
Up north we use our fists instead of knives.
I hope Benito's not dodging around some old grindstone
in the hold, and sharpening a knife for me.
Here, Perkins, help our men up the ladder.

[*Two immaculate* AMERICAN SAILORS *appear carrying great
casks of water. Two more follow carrying net baskets of wilted
pumpkins. The* NEGROES *begin to crowd forward, shouting,
"We want Yankee food, we want Yankee drink!"* DELANO
grandiosely holds up a pumpkin; an OLD NEGRO *rushes forward, snatches at the pumpkin, and knocks* DELANO *off-balance
into* PERKINS'S *arms.* DELANO *gets up and knocks the* NEGRO
down with his fist. All is tense and quiet. The SIX HATCHET-
CLEANERS *lift their hatchets above their heads*]

DELANO

[*Furious*]

Americans, stand by me! Stand by your captain!

[*Like lightning, the* AMERICANS *unsling their muskets, fix bayonets, and kneel with their guns pointing at the* NEGROES]

Don Benito, Sir, call your men to order!

BABU

We're starving, Yankee Master. We mean no harm;
we've never been so scared.

You try my patience, Babu.
I am talking to Captain Cereno;
call your men to order, Sir.

BENITO

Make them laugh, Babu. The Americans aren't going
   to shoot.

   [BABU *airily waves a hand. The* NEGROES *smile.* DELANO *turns
   to* BENITO]

You mustn't blame them too much; they're sick
   and hungry.
We have kept them cooped up for ages.

DELANO

   [*As the* NEGROES *relax*]

Form them in lines, Perkins!
Each man shall have his share.
That's how we run things in the States—
to each man equally, no matter what his claims.

NEGROES

   [*Standing back, bleating like sheep*]

Feed me, Master Yankee! Feed me, Master Yankee!

DELANO

You are much too close.
Here, Perkins, take the provisions aft.
You'll save lives by giving each as little as you can,
Be sure to keep a tally.

[FRANCESCO, *a majestic, yellow-colored mulatto, comes up to* DELANO]

FRANCESCO

My master requests your presence at dinner, Don Amasa.

DELANO

Tell him I have indigestion.
Tell him to keep better order on his ship.
It's always the man of good will that gets hurt;
my fist still aches from hitting that old darky.

FRANCESCO

My master has his own methods of discipline
that are suitable for our unfortunate circumstances.
Will you come to dinner, Don Amasa?

DELANO

I'll come. When in Rome, do as the Romans.
Excuse my quick temper, Sir.
It's better to blow up than to smoulder.

> [*The scrim curtain is raised. In the cabin, a long table loaded with silver has been laid out. The locker has been closed and the Spanish flag hangs on the wall.* DON BENITO *is seated,* BABU *stands behind him. As soon as* DELANO *sits down,* FRANCESCO *begins serving with great dignity and agility*]

FRANCESCO

A finger bowl, Don Amasa.

> [*After each statement, he moves about the table*]

A napkin, Don Amasa.
A glass of American water, Don Amasa.

A slice of American pumpkin, Don Amasa.
A goblet of American cider, Don Amasa.

[DELANO *drinks a great deal of cider,* BENITO *hardly touches his*]

DELANO

This is very courtly for a sick ship, Don Benito.
The Spanish Empire will never go down, if she keeps
    her chin up.

BENITO

I'm afraid I shan't live long enough to enjoy
    your prophecy.

DELANO

I propose a toast to the Spanish Empire
on which the sun never sets;
may you find her still standing, when you land, Sir!

BENITO

Our Empire has lasted three hundred years,
I suppose she will last another month.
I wish I could say the same for myself. My sun is setting,
I hear the voices of the dead in this calm.

DELANO

You hear the wind lifting;
it's bringing our two vessels together.
We are going to take you into port, Don Benito.

BENITO

You are either too late or too early with your good works.

Our yellow fever may break out again.
You aren't going to put your men in danger, Don Amasa?

DELANO

My boys are all healthy, sir.

BENITO

Health isn't God, I wouldn't trust it.

FRANCESCO

May I fill your glass, Don Amasa?

BABU

New wine in new bottles,
that's the American spirit, Yankee Master.
They say all men are created equal in North America.

DELANO

We prefer merit to birth, boy.

[BABU *motions imperiously for* FRANCESCO *to leave. As he goes,
bowing to the* CAPTAINS, FOUR NEGROES *play the* Marseillaise]

Why are they playing the *Marseillaise?*

BABU

His uncle is supposed to have been in the
        French Convention,
and voted for the death of the French King.

DELANO

This polite and royal fellow is no anarchist!

BABU

Francesco is very *ancien regime,*
he is even frightened of the Americans.

He doesn't like the way you treated King George.
Babu is more liberal.

DELANO

A royal fellow,
this usher of yours, Don Benito!
He is as yellow as a goldenrod.
He is a king, a king of kind hearts.
What a pleasant voice he has!

BENITO

[*Glumly*]

Francesco is a good man.

DELANO

As long as you've known him,
he's been a worthy fellow, hasn't he?
Tell me, I am particularly curious to know.

BENITO

Francesco is a good man.

DELANO

I'm glad to hear it, I am glad to hear it!
You refute the saying of a planter friend of mine.
He said, "When a mulatto has a regular European face,
look out for him, he is a devil."

BENITO

I've heard your planter's remark applied
to intermixtures of Spaniards and Indians;
I know nothing about mulattoes.

174

DELANO

No, no, my friend's refuted;
if we're so proud of our white blood,
surely a little added to the blacks improves their breed.
I congratulate you on your servants, Sir.

BABU

We've heard that Jefferson, the King of your Republic,
would like to free his slaves.

DELANO

Jefferson has read too many books, boy,
but you can trust him. He's a gentleman and an American!
He's not lifting a finger to free his slaves.

BABU

We hear you have a new capital modelled on Paris,
and that your President is going to set up
a guillotine on the Capitol steps.

DELANO

Oh, Paris! I told you you could trust Mr. Jefferson, boy,
he stands for law and order like your mulatto.
Have you been to Paris, Don Benito?

BENITO

I'm afraid I'm just a provincial Spaniard, Captain.

DELANO

Let me tell you about Paris.
You know what French women are like—
nine parts sex and one part logic.
Well, one of them in Paris heard

that my ship was the *President Adams*. She said,
"You are descended from Adam, Captain,
you must know everything,
tell me how Adam and Eve learned to sleep together."
Do you know what I said?

BENITO

No, Captain.

DELANO

I said, "I guess Eve was a Frenchwoman,
the first Frenchwoman."
Do you know what she answered?

BENITO

No, Captain Delano.

DELANO

She said, "I was trying to provoke a philosophical
    discussion, Sir."
A philosophical discussion, ha, ha!
You look serious, Sir. You know, something troubles me.

BENITO

Something troubles you, Captain Delano?

DELANO

I still can't understand those calms,
but let that go. The scurvy,
why did it kill off three Spaniards in every four,
and only half the blacks?

Benito Cereno

Negroes are human, but surely you couldn't have
    favored them
before your own flesh and blood!

BENITO

This is like the Inquisition, Captain Delano.
I have done the best I could.

[BABU *dabs* BENITO's *forehead with cider*]

BABU

Poor, poor Master; since Don Aranda died,
he trusts no one except Babu.

DELANO

Your Babu is an uncommonly intelligent fellow;
you are right to trust him, Sir.
Sometimes I think we overdo our talk of freedom.
If you looked into our hearts, we all want slaves.

BENITO

Disease is a mysterious thing;
it takes one man, and leaves his friend.
Only the unfortunate can understand misfortune.

DELANO

I must return to my bosun;
he's pretty green to be left alone here.
Before I go I want to propose a last toast to you!
A good master deserves good servants!

[*He gets up. As he walks back to* PERKINS, *the scrim curtain falls, concealing* BENITO *and* BABU]

That captain must have jaundice,
I wish he kept better order.
I don't like hitting menials.

PERKINS

I've done some looking around, Sir. I've used my eyes.

DELANO

That's what they're for, I guess. You have to watch
    your step,
this hulk, this rotten piece of finery,
will fall apart. This old world needs new blood
and Yankee gunnery to hold it up.
You shouldn't mess around, though, it's their ship;
you're breaking all the laws of the sea.

PERKINS

Do you see that man-shaped thing in canvas?

DELANO

I see it.

PERKINS

Behind the cloth, there's a real skeleton,
a man dressed up like Don Benito.

DELANO

They're Catholics, and worship bones.

PERKINS

There's writing on its coat. It says,
"I am Don Aranda," and, "Follow your leader."

178

DELANO

Follow your leader?

PERKINS

I saw two blacks unfurling a flag,
a black skull and crossbones on white silk.

DELANO

That's piracy. We've been ordered
to sink any ship that flies that flag.
Perhaps they were playing.

PERKINS

I saw King Atufal throw away his chains,
He called for food, the Spaniards served him two pieces
     of pumpkin,
and a whole bottle of your cider.

DELANO

Don Benito has the only key to Atufal's padlock.
My cider was for the captain's table.

PERKINS

Atufal pointed to the cabin where you were dining,
and drew a finger across his throat.

DELANO

Who could want to kill Amasa Delano?

PERKINS

I warned our men to be ready for an emergency.

DELANO

You're a mind reader,

I couldn't have said better myself;
but we're at peace with Spain.

PERKINS

I told them to return with loaded muskets
and fixed bayonets.

DELANO

Here comes Benito. Watch how I'll humor him
and sound him out.

[BABU *brings out* BENITO's *chair.* BENITO *sits in it*]

It's good to have you back on deck, Captain.
Feel the breeze! It holds and will increase.
My ship is moving nearer. Soon we will be together.
We have seen you through your troubles.

BENITO

Remember, I warned you about the yellow fever.
I am surprised you haven't felt afraid.

DELANO

Oh, that will blow away.
Everything is going to go better and better;
the wind's increasing, soon you'll have no cares.
After the long voyage, the anchor drops into the harbor.
It's a great weight lifted from the captain's heart.
We are getting to be friends, Don Benito.
My ship's in sight, the *President Adams!*
How the wind braces a man up!
I have a small invitation to issue to you.

BENITO

An invitation?

DELANO

I want you to take a cup of coffee
with me on my quarter deck tonight.
The Sultan of Turkey never tasted such coffee
as my old steward makes. What do you say, Don Benito?

BENITO

I cannot leave my ship.

DELANO

Come, come, you need a change of climate.
The sky is suddenly blue, Sir,
my coffee will make a man of you.

BENITO

I cannot leave my ship.
Even now, I don't think you understand my position here.

DELANO

I want to speak to you alone.

BENITO

I am alone, as much as I ever am.

DELANO

In America, we don't talk about money
in front of servants and children.

BENITO

Babu is not my servant.
You spoke of money—since the yellow fever,

he has had a better head for figures than I have.

DELANO

You embarrass me, Captain,
but since circumstances are rather special here,
I will proceed.

BENITO

Babu takes an interest in all our expenses.

DELANO

Yes, I am going to talk to you about your expenses.
I am responsible to my owners for all
the sails, ropes, food and carpentry I give you.
You will need a complete rerigging, almost a new ship,
    in fact,
You shall have our services at cost.

BENITO

I know, you are a merchant.
I suppose I ought to pay you for our lives.

DELANO

I envy you, Captain. You are the only owner
of the *San Domingo,* since Don Aranda died.
I am just an employee. Our owners would sack me,
if I followed my better instincts.

BENITO

You can give your figures to Babu, Captain.

DELANO

You are very offhand about money, Sir;

182

I don't think you realize the damage that has been done
    to your ship.
Ah, you smile. I'm glad you're loosening up.
Look, the water gurgles merrily, the wind is high,
a mild light is shining. I sometimes think
such a tropical light as this must have shone
on the tents of Abraham and Isaac.
It seems as if Providence were watching over us.

PERKINS

There are things that need explaining here, Sir.

DELANO

Yes, Captain, Perkins saw some of your men
unfurling an unlawful flag,
a black skull and crossbones.

BENITO

You know my only flag is the Lion and Castle of Spain.

DELANO

No, Perkins says he saw a skull and crossbones.
That's piracy. I trust Perkins.
You've heard about how my government blew
the bowels out of the pirates at Tripoli?

BENITO

Perhaps my Negroes . . .

DELANO

My government doesn't intend
to let you play at piracy!

BENITO

Perhaps my Negroes were playing.
When you take away their chains . . .

DELANO

I'll see that you are all put back in chains,
if you start playing pirates!

PERKINS

There's something else he can explain, Sir.

DELANO

Yes, Perkins saw Atufal throw off his chains
and order dinner.

BABU

Master has the key, Yankee Master.

BENITO

I have the key.
You can't imagine how my position exhausts me, Captain.

DELANO

I can imagine. Atufal's chains are fakes.
You and he are in cahoots, Sir!

PERKINS

They don't intend to pay for our sails and service.
They think America is Santa Claus.

DELANO

The United States are death on pirates and debtors.

PERKINS

There's one more thing for him to explain, Sir.

DELANO

Do you see that man-shaped thing covered with black
    cloth, Don Benito?

BENITO

I always see it.

DELANO

Take away the cloth. I order you to take away the cloth!

BENITO

I cannot. Oh, Santa Maria, have mercy!

DELANO

Of course, you can't. It's no Virgin Mary.
You have done something terrible to your friend,
    Don Aranda.
Take away the cloth, Perkins!

[*As* PERKINS *moves forward,* ATUFAL *suddenly stands chainless
and with folded arms, blocking his way*]

BABU

[*Dancing up and down and beside himself*]

Let them see it! Let them see it!
I can't stand any more of their insolence;
the Americans treat us like their slaves!

[BABU *and* PERKINS *meet at the man-shaped object and start
pulling away the cloth.* BENITO *rushes between them, and
throws them back and sprawling on the deck.* BABU *and* PER-
KINS *rise, and stand hunched like wrestlers, about to close in
on* BENITO, *who draws his sword with a great gesture. It is only
a hilt. He runs at* BABU *and knocks him down.* ATUFAL *throws*

off his chains and signals to the HATCHET-CLEANERS. *They stand behind* BENITO *with raised hatchets. The* NEGROES *shout ironically, "Evviva Benito!"*]

You too, Yankee Captain!
If you shoot, we'll kill you.

DELANO

If a single American life is lost,
I will send this ship to the bottom,
and all Peru after it.
Do you hear me, Don Benito?

BENITO

Don't you understand? I am as powerless as you are!

BABU

He is as powerless as you are.

BENITO

Don't you understand? He has been holding a knife at
    my back.
I have been talking all day to save your life.

BABU

    [*Holding a whip*]

Do you see this whip? When Don Aranda was out
    of temper,
he used to snap pieces of flesh off us with it.
Now I hold the whip.
When I snap it, Don Benito jumps!

    [*Snaps the whip.* DON BENITO *flinches*]

186

DELANO

[*Beginning to understand*]

It's easy to terrorize the defenseless.

BABU

That's what we thought when Don Aranda held the whip.

DELANO

You'll find I am made of tougher stuff than your Spaniards.

ATUFAL

We want to kill you.

NEGROES

We want to kill you, Yankee Captain.

DELANO

Who could want to kill Amasa Delano?

BABU

Of course. We want to keep you alive.
We want you to sail us back to Africa.
Has anyone told you how much you are worth, Captain?

DELANO

I have another course in mind.

BENITO

Yes, there's another course if you don't like Africa, there's
    another course.
King Atufal, show the Yankee captain
the crew that took the other course!

[*Three dead* SPANISH SAILORS *are brought on stage*]

187

ATUFAL

Look at Don Aranda?

DELANO

Yes, you are hot-tempered and discourteous, Captain.
I am going to introduce you to Don Aranda.
You have a new command, Captain. You must meet your
    new owner.

> [*The black cloth is taken from the man-shaped object and
> shows a chalk-white skeleton dressed like* DON BENITO]

Don Amasa, Don Aranda!
You can see that Don Aranda was a white man like you,
because his bones are white.

NEGROES

He is a white because his bones are white!
He is a white because his bones are white!

ATUFAL

> [*Pointing to the ribbon on the skeleton's chest*]

Do you see that ribbon?
It says, "Follow the leader."
We wrote it in his blood.

BABU

He was a white man
even though his blood was red as ours.

NEGROES

He is white because his bones are white!

BABU

Don Aranda is our figurehead,
we are going to chain him to the bow of our ship
to scare off devils.

BABU

This is the day of Jubilee,
I am raising the flag of freedom!

NEGROES

Freedom! Freedom! Freedom!

> [*The black skull and crossbones is raised on two poles. The* NEGROES *form two lines, leading up to the flag, and leave an aisle. Each man is armed with some sort of weapon*]

BABU

Spread out the Spanish flag!

> [*The Lion and Castle of Spain is spread out on the deck in front of the skull and crossbones*]

The Spanish flag is the road to freedom.
Don Benito mustn't hurt his white feet on the splinters.

> [*Kneeling in front of* BENITO]

Your foot, Master!

> [BENITO *holds out his foot.* BABU *takes off* BENITO's *shoes*]

Give Don Benito back his sword!

> [*The sword-hilt is fastened back in* BENITO's *scabbard*]

Load him with chains!

> [*Two heavy chains are draped on* BENITO's *neck. The cane and ball are handed to him*]

Former Captain Benito Cereno, kneel!
Ask pardon of man!

BENITO

> [*Kneeling*]

I ask pardon for having been born a Spaniard.
I ask pardon for having enslaved my fellow man.

BABU

Strike off the oppressor's chain!

> [*One of* BENITO's *chains is knocked off, then handed to* ATU-
> FAL, *who dashes it to the deck*]

Former Captain Benito Cereno,
you must kiss the flag of freedom.

> [*Points to* DON ARANDA]

Kiss the mouth of the skull!

> [BENITO *walks barefoot over the Spanish flag and kisses the
> mouth of* DON ARANDA]

NEGROES

Evviva Benito! Evviva Benito!

> [*Sounds are heard from* PERKINS, *whose head is still covered
> with the sack*]

ATUFAL

The bosun wants to kiss the mouth of freedom.

BABU

March over the Spanish flag, Bosun.

> [PERKINS *starts forward*]

DELANO

You are dishonoring your nation, Perkins!
Don't you stand for anything?

PERKINS

I only have one life, Sir.

[*Walks over the Spanish flag and kisses the mouth of the skull*]

NEGROES

Evviva Bosun! *Evviva* Bosun!

DELANO

You are no longer an American, Perkins!

BABU

He was free to choose freedom, Captain.

ATUFAL

Captain Delano wants to kiss the mouth of freedom.

BABU

He is jealous of the bosun.

ATUFAL

In the United States, all men are created equal.

BABU

Don't you want to kiss the mouth of freedom, Captain?

DELANO

[*Lifting his pocket and pointing the pistol*]

Do you see what I have in my hand?

BABU

A pistol.

DELANO

I am unable to miss at this distance.

BABU

You must take your time, Yankee Master.
You must take your time.

DELANO

I am unable to miss.

BABU

You can stand there like a block of wood
as long as you want to, Yankee Master.
You will drop asleep, then we will tie you up,
and make you sail us back to Africa.

> [*General laughter. Suddenly, there's a roar of gunfire. Several* NEGROES, *mostly women, fall.* AMERICAN SEAMAN *in spotless blue and white throw themselves in a lying position on deck.* MORE *kneel above them, then* MORE *stand above these. All have muskets and fixed bayonets. The First Row fires. More* NEGROES *fall. They start to retreat. The Second Row fires. More* NEGROES *fall. They retreat further. The Third Row fires. The Three* AMERICAN LINES *march forward, but all the* NE-GROES *are either dead or in retreat.* DON BENITO *has been wounded. He staggers over to* DELANO *and shakes his hand*]

BENITO

You have saved my life.
I thank you for my life.

192

DELANO

A man can only do what he can,
We have saved American lives.

PERKINS

[*Pointing to* ATUFAL'S *body*]

We have killed King Atufal,
we have killed their ringleader.

[BABU *jumps up. He is unwounded*]

BABU

I was the King. Babu, not Atufal
was the king, who planned, dared and carried out
the seizure of this ship, the *San Domingo*.
Untouched by blood myself, I had all
the most dangerous and useless Spaniards killed.
I freed my people from their Egyptian bondage.
The heartless Spaniards slaved for me like slaves.

[BABU *steps back, and quickly picks up a crown from the litter*]

This is my crown.

[*Puts crown on his head. He snatches* BENITO'S *rattan cane*]

This is my rod.

[*Picks up silver ball*]

This is the earth.

[*Holds the ball out with one hand and raises the cane*]

This is the arm of the angry God.

[*Smashes the ball*]

193

PERKINS

Let him surrender. Let him surrender.
We want to save someone.

BENITO

My God how little these people understand!

BABU

[*Holding a white handkerchief and raising both his hands*]

Yankee Master understand me. The future is with us.

DELANO

[*Raising his pistol*]

This is your future.

[BABU *falls and lies still.* DELANO *pauses, then slowly empties the five remaining barrels of his pistol into the body. Lights dim*]

CURTAIN